FEARFUL *to* fabulous

Advance Praise

"A very good read for dealing with a traumatic situation. Fiona Eckersly provides a helpful guide and roadmap for addressing the trauma of divorce. Her heartfelt personal perspective on the topic will help the reader transform their situation into a positive, life-changing experience. Her practical, "tell it like it is" style coupled with her personal story and other real-life situations is effective and inspiring. As an individual and family health coach and wellness educator, I highly recommend this book to anyone dealing with the emotional trials and aftermath of divorce."

– Sue Zook, Ed. D.

"Fearful to Fabulous is both a love letter and a helpful guide to women going through divorce after long marriages from someone who's been there. It covers all of the areas—finances, self-identity, friendships, and more—that get thrown into disarray from a midlife divorce. It has helpful exercises and techniques, and it absolutely shows you that you're not alone, that someone understands what you're going through, and that others have gone through it and found their way to a better sense of themselves and a better life—and so can you."

– Lisa Nichols

FEARFUL
to fabulous

Unlock Your Power, Move On,
and Thrive After Midlife Divorce

FIONA ECKERSLEY

NEW YORK

LONDON • NASHVILLE • MELBOURNE • VANCOUVER

FEARFUL *to* fabulous
Unlock Your Power, Move On, and Thrive After Midlife Divorce

© 2020 **FIONA ECKERSLEY**

Published in New York, New York, by Morgan James Publishing in partnership with Difference Press. Morgan James is a trademark of Morgan James, LLC. www.MorganJamesPublishing.com

ISBN 978-1-64279-703-9 paperback
ISBN 978-1-64279-704-6 eBook
ISBN 978-1-64279-705-3 Audio
Library of Congress Control Number: 2019908761

Cover Design by:
Megan Whitney
megan@creativeninjadesigns.com

Interior Design by:
Bonnie Bushman
The Whole Caboodle Graphic Design

Morgan James is a proud partner of Habitat for Humanity Peninsula and Greater Williamsburg. Partners in building since 2006.

Get involved today! Visit
www.MorganJamesBuilds.com

The four most important people in this world should know that if you really want it, then don't let anything, including yourself, get in the way.

Table of Contents

Introduction

When it comes down to it, I really want to use this book in order to reach a greater audience of women who have found themselves struggling with the challenges brought on by their midlife divorce. Whether they were the instigators, or they were blindsided by this new life situation they find themselves in, they feel as if they are in some kind of limbo—unable to let go of the past and what might have been yet yearning to move on and start a new life in which they can feel control and happiness. They can use this book as a tool to stop spinning in the uncertainty, something to help them move on and thrive in this new adventure after their marriage has ended. So many of the women that I have talked to over the years really wanted to go through to the next stage but have been held back by the fear of what it might take to get there. Or they've been paralyzed by the belief that they couldn't possibly do that. My hope is that this book can help them to take the first steps on that journey. I also want to be an inspiration by showing that none of us are alone in this situation. It is possible to move on from this. Not only move on but even feel happier and more at peace than you actually were in your marriage. It is so sad to think of so many women that are tied to the negative emotions and the false beliefs about themselves. Not only does that put them into the situations they find themselves in now, but it is stopping them from moving on at all. So many women repeat the same mistakes and end up with the same toxic patterns in their next relationships. I should know; I lived my pattern over and over until I was able to finally break free. The self-blame and loathing that so many women go through every day is just so unnecessary! One of my biggest wishes for my readers is that the advice in this book will stop that from happening to them.

To be honest, working with my clients and writing this book been extremely cathartic for me too. Every day as I am talking, I find inspiration from the women that are working so diligently to change their lives for the better. Sometimes I actually feel as if what I am saying to them isn't even coming from me but is coming to me. Subtle difference but a huge one nonetheless!

Of course, I had come a long way in order to do this line of work in the first place, but it has propelled me to a further understanding of things about myself and my life including my marriage and relationships that I had not fully investigated before.

I also found that the more I work with my clients, the more my approach to what they actually need has changed. It started off as just how to get past the immediate problems of suddenly seeing your future disappear and wondering what you were going to do now. Now I see that this has been an issue of a lifelong problem for many, myself included, that has suddenly been outed by the divorce and the need to face realities that you maybe rather wouldn't.

I have been amazed by how many of the women are so angry that the man left them, but in actual fact, they had lived walking on eggshells and pretty unhappy for many years. What they say to themselves once they have been released from this is that they must have done something wrong or they should have tried harder to fix it, and so this whole situation is really their fault. Like the joke around our house that of course... "It's All Mom's Fault."

Their boundaries are gone but were so slowly eroded that they had not even noticed until they are alone. The bar for the way they should be treated is incredibly low. It's like the frog in the slowly boiling pot. As they look back, many still have an unrealistic, fairy-tale view of what their actual marriage was like. They say that it came as a huge shock. Amy had told me that she had spoken to her husband about his apparent friendship with the young woman in his office but in the next breath said that she had no earthly idea that he would do such a thing as cheat on her. Clearly if she had been honest with herself at the time, she would have seen that something was amiss. It is so easy for the women I talk with to blame themselves when the husband has an affair. I want you to know if you are reading this book that it actually has nothing to do with you at all, although the man in your life may say differently. Men can (and will) be very cruel to cover up their misdeeds and push the blame onto the woman. Poor Kathleen lived over and over the remark from her husband as she was dressing one morning that she really did nothing for him. In the end, how you look, or think you look, is not the factor. It is that he feels he needs more to make him feel better. That is caused by the hole inside of him and can only be fixed by him.

This book is to celebrate who you are now and the fabulous woman that you will become. It is time to stop looking back at the past and what might have been! That was not meant to be. Following the steps in this book will let you release the past. It will allow you to find a new understanding of the events in your life thus far. Using this knowledge, you will then be able to find the self-confidence to outline your goals and plan out the next steps on your journey. This next phase of your life will, I believe, be the best yet.

—**Fiona**

{ **Chapter 1**
Now What? }

It was so hard to hear those words come out of his mouth. You didn't think that it would really come to this, that he doesn't want to try any more, that he thinks that you will both be much better off when this whole thing is over. The kids will be fine, he said. They are resilient, everyone knows that, he said. He didn't seem to be considering if *you* would be fine. He told you that has been feeling this way for a long time now and his mind is made up. Apparently, you didn't get to have a say in how the rest of your life was going to go. So, you went through your days, slightly tearful, slightly numb, groggy from

1

lack of sleep. You needed to be there for the kids. You couldn't look to be falling apart. So, you kept it all together, at least on the outside. There was so much to do. You had to figure out how much you spend every month on clothes for the kids, haircuts, dog grooming—for goodness sake! Making decisions that couldn't be pushed aside or not delved into because your lawyer was telling you that we need them next week, yesterday. Dates and deadlines and meetings to get to and through. You had to keep going. There wasn't time to spend thinking too much about the future. Then the big day arrived. Not the other big day where you had been surrounded by friends and family. Not the other big day that you had celebrated a lifetime ago. This day you are going in there by yourself. This day was the day you signed the papers, and the years of togetherness, of being a family, are suddenly all wiped out like it didn't really matter to him in the first place.

You signed those papers.

Now what?

Now you are not part of a couple. Now you have to go to parties by yourself or sit at home with a glass of wine wondering if he was invited. Now you can't help thinking that he is having a much better time in his new life without you. Now you are a single mother. You are going to have to drive to all of those games for both kids, even if they happen at the same time. You are going to have to be the one to impose curfew and deal with it when she comes home at midnight. You are going to have to mow the lawn by yourself. You are going to have to get an emergency plumber to come over when water suddenly starts pouring through the kitchen ceiling. You need to actually figure out what that homeowners policy covers. You are going to have to take a hard look at the budget and make sure that you can cover the mortgage this week. You have to tell everyone that you got divorced. You have to see the judgement in their eyes. Now no one is pushing you, and you have time to think about this. You feel totally alone.

Karen is a kindergarten teacher who lives in Connecticut. She is fifty-two years old and was married to her husband for twenty-five years before they got divorced. She has three children, two girls and a boy. Her oldest, Cindy, has finished college and lives about two hours away working at an office job. Jenny is still a sophomore in college, and her son Ben is a senior in high school. The kids are feeling quite resentful about the divorce and are all handling it in different ways. They don't really know who they should blame or be loyal to and kind of wish that they could ignore the whole thing and just get on with their own lives. They don't want to get involved, they say. But in reality, they are having a very hard time coping with this new situation. Her son is having the most difficult time. He feels abandoned by his father and is acting out. His grades are not as good as they used to be, and she isn't sure what will happen about college next year. He won't talk to her about it at all and is refusing to go to therapy. Karen feels like she is coping with this problem alone because he lives with her most of the time and his moodiness, reckless behavior, and lack of respect for her house rules is a constant source of conflict in the house.

She did not initiate the divorce, and it actually came as a shock to her because he had never mentioned that he would go that far. She couldn't believe that he would do such a thing to her after she had basically done everything for him and the kids in the marriage. She is so confused about what she could have done to prevent the breakup, and it makes her very sad that this has happened. She feels that she should have done more to keep everyone together.

Added to all this, he has already moved on with a new girlfriend. They are living in a lovely house and seem to be having a wonderful life, while Karen is struggling to deal with the kids and her new life. She can't stop thinking about her ex and the life that they had had all planned out. She just feels so angry all the time. Why did he do this to her?

She still lives in the very nice five-bedroom house in the suburbs that she was in when married, but she is very worried about how she will stay there because money is much tighter than it was before, and a teacher's salary won't come near to covering the expenses. Her alimony is helping, but she isn't sure how far that will go. The kids have big expenses now like cars and college costs, but they are older, so those expenses were not considered when she got divorced.

Some of the friends that they had as a couple are going out with Karen's ex and his new girlfriend, and she finds this very difficult to understand. Many of her other friends have just sort of faded out. She did go on a couple of girl's nights out with them at the beginning, but it was clear that they were feeling a little awkward, and she felt uncomfortable around them. She feels very lonely and doesn't know how to make friends.

Karen tried a couple of dating sites as friends said she should move on and get a boyfriend. She did go on a couple of dates and even went out with one guy several times. None of them seemed that nice once she got to know them.

Work is not going well as she isn't sleeping, and her emotions are all over the place. She has become distracted and even a little short with the class at times. She hates that and is so angry at herself that she can't seem to hold it together. Added to all that is the fact that she has put on about twenty-five pounds in the last year or so. The harder she tries to lose it, the more she puts on.

It is really hard for her to make any kind of decision. She doesn't remember being like that before, but now she is always second guessing herself. Sometimes she finds that she is just sitting on the couch when she knows she has many things to do, but she can't seem to choose what to do first and so in the end nothing gets done. She feels like such a fat, lazy loser!

Karen finds that she is always worried about what people are thinking. It seems that she imagines everyone judging her all the time. But when she has moments of honesty with herself, she is judging herself. How could she be such a failure?

Many of the women I speak to after their divorce feel exactly the same way as Karen does—the anger and frustration that they are constantly feeling. It swings between blaming their ex-husband or themselves for not getting through this in a better way, angry that this could even happen, and they feel lonely. The greater weight they feel every day is fear, a fear of the future and how they are going to manage in so many different areas of their life: finances, career, love life, kids, the fear that they will be alone like this forever.

When you have been doing so much for so many others for so long, being faced with time to reflect upon who you are and what you want can cause frustrations all of its own. If your identity was tied to the marriage and husband and children, who are you now?

The anxiety, stress, roller coaster ride of emotions, and lack of sleep from all of that can take a huge toll on your health. New physical symptoms like stomach issues, pains in your shoulders, headaches, and constant fatigue can seem to pop up out of nowhere, adding more stress to the mix.

It all seems like there can be no way out of this place you find yourself in now. If, like Karen, it is all too overwhelming, then I want you to know that you are never alone in this. There is support all around you from others that have gone through this and come out the other side to find a secure and fabulous future, one where they are calm and in control, one where there is laughter and friendships and everyday joy. There is a path to this place if you are ready move on. It doesn't matter if you have been waiting for a week or ten years to move on because once you feel that this is your time, it can be done. Once you are ready to get out of the pain that you have been living in, push out of the comfort zone, and start to focus on the solution, then you are on your way to your fabulous future.

Instead, you can turn around those fears you had after you signed the papers to see a more positive future.

Now you are free to find a relationship where you are valued. Now you are able to choose friends who support and inspire you. You make decisions about the way you want to live your life. You have the opportunity to show your children that anything is possible if you believe in yourself. You are going to learn how to communicate with your children so that they can gain independence while having respect for your rules. You are going to find strengths that you never realized you had. You can finally understand that you can manage finances on your own. You can learn to budget and appreciate all the great things you have in your life already. You can show everyone that you are a strong independent woman. You can see that friends may be living in a situation that is not as perfect as they would have had you believe, because they were afraid to admit it. You have the time to look at your life and decide what goals you want to set for yourself. You can find a new tribe of supportive women who have been through what you have and let you know that life is good.

I know that you can do this. I believe in you, even if you're not quite there yet to believe in yourself. I have a really good reason for that. I know that you can do this because I did it. I have seen my clients do it. They are women of different ages, from all walks of life and different parts of the country. The thing they have in common is their desire to move on from the place of fear to the place of happiness, security, and control.

Sheila had not seen how she had been unable to stop being the caretaker for her ex-husband even long after the divorce. As she shared with me after we had worked together, "I was able to get clearer on where I am and where I want to go. I was able to emotionally be divorced, which I wasn't sure I could do. I learned a lot about myself in the process. This is not about staying in the past or pain; it's about finding yourself in the middle of all that! Being able to quickly see what needs work and take active steps to get there. I'm in a much better place emotionally, able to have distance and separation from my ex but also have better boundaries or insight on why I may have issues setting them. Ready to move forward with whatever comes next, not feeling stuck."

Ready?

Chapter 2
How Did I Get Here?

"There will come a time when you believe
everything is finished, that will be the beginning."
– Louis L'Amour

If I really sat down to analyze it, I suppose I was, at that point in time, feeling stressed out and walking on eggshells. I was wondering what was going to be the thing that I had done this time to disappoint, anger, or upset him. Things had been feeling strange for a few days, and as he walked into the bedroom, I thought that I was finally going to find out what it was, only the words that came out of his mouth were so not the words that I had been expecting to hear. Never in a million years would I have thought that he would say something like that. I thought we had the perfect family and life. Yes, I supposed there were quite a few things that I was holding back that I was not really happy about. That was how a marriage is though, right? I couldn't expect to be blissfully happy; that was a myth for the movies. Putting up with the things that bothered me was just the way it went, I thought. This is as it would always be—things progressing as they do until monotony and old age, us settled into that grumpy old couple that barely even spoke but celebrated every anniversary with all the kids gathered round the cake, then the retirement place wherever he had dreamed it would be, of course. But, you know, my kids would be happy and successful. I basically had no decisions to make. I was secure. So on and so on until one of us dropped dead. Isn't that how it is all supposed to work? So, yes, I might have been a little snippy and bitter and sometimes maybe pissed people off just for fun. It was certainly better than the marriages that I had seen all around me growing up. Then again, it wasn't the interesting life I had envisioned when we met: traveling the globe, working to help those in dire need. It wasn't so much about feeling great emotions or getting a say in what I did or who I had as a best friend or even what I could comfortably express with my words. It was a tradeoff that I was apparently willing to make. But now, here it was. That choice was taken out of my hands. It was no longer up to me.

"I don't love you anymore, and I'm filing for divorce," he said.

He said it, and I was suddenly numb.

It was an unbelievable statement, yet there it was. I had to believe it because he had just said it. He, who had never actually communicated very much at all (biggest issue really, our non-communication), was suddenly as clear and concise as a bell. He left pretty much no doubt that the whole future I'd been holding onto—good, bad, boring, safe, or secure—had evaporated.

Was I sad, happy, angry…? I don't know what I was because there were no sensations. As thought did finally come back and I was about to ask the questions that had come into my head, my little girl walked into the room. He left. The message was delivered, and the moment had passed. The incendiary message that not only blew up my world, my view of myself, and my future but which would progress to fundamentally changing who I was, who I wanted to be, and who I still continue to become.

That was the five-minute window when I found out that I would be a divorced woman in her forties. The story of how I got there could honestly fill another couple of books in themselves. So, I'll save much of it for those.

I grew up in an industrial town in the North of England. I went to college. I was the first and only person in my family to do that. To be truthful about it, I went not because I was encouraged and pushed to do so by my family but because it was the only way I could see to get out of my childhood home. I became a teacher and after graduation went to teach for a charity organization in Sierra Leone, West Africa. I met my husband there because he was in the Peace Corps. I was teaching in the same village as he was. I moved to New York to be with him when that was done. Time passed, and there I was in the suburbs, married with four children.

He had a large, close-knit family who lived in the same town. We had a beautiful house on a quiet cul-de-sac where all the neighbors got together and had fun. For all intents and purposes, our life was totally idyllic, the perfect family. Then sometime after our seventeenth wedding anniversary, twenty-two years into our being together, that message was delivered.

When my children did eventually find out that we were getting a divorce, it was extremely hard for them. We had all seemed so perfectly happy. There had been no indication that mum and dad were having problems. There were certainly no loud arguments. Quiet fuming would be how I can describe it now. Aged fifteen, thirteen, eleven, and eight at the time, their world was absolutely destroyed.

My parents were dead, and I had really not been very close to them truthfully. My siblings were in the U.K. The family I had been close to for twenty years were actually my in laws. Suddenly, they were not my family any more. No more large Christmas or Thanksgiving gatherings for me.

Many of the friends we had as a couple were people he had grown up with or gone to college with. The friends I did have left were all part of a couple.

What I did know was that I couldn't take to my bed and pull the covers up over my head. I had four kids to take care of. So I got up every day and methodically went through the steps that I thought I should. Focusing on the divorce process actually helped to pull me through. There were steps laid out for me that I needed to take. But once that was done with, I was lost. Friends would regularly comment to me that they didn't know how I could do so well. What they didn't know was that, at the time, the inside did not match the outside. There were moments when I would suddenly start to feel it hard to breathe as I was going about my day. I recognized that this was a panic attack, as I had been thinking about my future and the overwhelming decisions that seemed to stretch out in front of me.

This uncertainty drained my confidence in myself and my judgement. I can honestly say that I made some spectacularly bad decisions along the way.

My lowest point came a few years after my divorce. Having gone through some more prolonged legal battles with my ex-husband, I was feeling bitter and angry, something I had vowed I would not become. My children were feeling the effects of our bad relationship. I didn't have a romantic relationship, and I was feeling alone and isolated. I was using food as medication, which was contributing even more to my low view of myself. I didn't even enjoy my teaching job anymore, and I was wondering what I was going to do to make ends meet once my alimony would run out. I had absolutely no idea what I was going to do. I also didn't have too much confidence that I was going to be able to figure it out.

Something that had happened in my life to add to my sense of not being able to trust myself was a long relationship that had started not too long after my divorce. As many of us do, I had thought that finding a new relationship was the way to heal my confidence in myself, and when I met a man who seemed to be so far from the person that my ex-husband was, it seemed to be a perfect match. He was charming and treated me like a princess, something that I had never experienced in my life up to that point. It seemed that finally here was someone who was going to look after everything and worship me and grow old together in a really fun way. If you knew me at all, then you knew that even thinking that is not within the normal parameters of my usual personality. This was a relationship that lasted on and off for more than four years. Looking back, I know now that two weeks into it I was seeing red flags that I know for sure, had I been on the outside, I would have told a friend to run as far away from him as possible. Yet, I ignored all of the signs and what my gut was telling me.

The eventual cost of all of that was emotional, financial, health, and damage to the relationships that I had with others—my children among them. My eventual need to have the local police involved convinced me that I needed to take a closer look at the boundaries that I was setting for myself in romantic relationships! In fact, this was such a wakeup call to me that it was like a physical blow. I have described it in the past as if someone had wacked me on the side of the head with a frying pan. I finally had some sense knocked into me! I would rather help others to avoid that mistake.

The idea that I needed to change careers is perhaps the second thing that spurred me out of my downward spiral. When you have so many decisions to make, it really does seem so much easier to sit on the couch and watch *My 600lb Life* or some other nonsense that requires no thought. The more you avoid, the more you feel bad about it, the more you berate yourself, the more you feel incapable of making any decent decisions!

My particular block was what was I going to do for the rest of my life? I really was drifting along, and after, a friend suggested looking up coaching as a possible career. I had no idea what she was talking about at the time. I figured that was not an actual real thing that people did. What it did lead to, however, was a real deep dive into who I was and what I believed.

The more I looked into ideas and concepts about emotional healing and mindset, the more I became fascinated by everything that went along with it. I sought out people that spent their lives studying and teaching these ideas, and I practiced, studied, read and got to know who I was. More importantly, who it was I wanted to be.

Eventually, I did enroll in a coaching certification program and continued to learn more about myself and how I could help others. Besides the women that I have worked with as private clients, I spoke to many, many women, for an hour at a time, who shared their stories with me. So many diverse stories but essentially, we all have commonalities that need to be brought out into the open and healed. Once this is done, I have been amazed at how rapidly they were able to face the future with a completely different outlook. Once we see the truth of who we are and stop paying attention to the negative inner voices that have been poured into us throughout our lifetimes, the possibilities are limitless.

{ Chapter 3 }
7 Vital Solution Steps

"As we know better, we do better."
– Maya Angelou

The emotional turmoil as the result of the major life transition of divorce is recognized by the Holmes and Rahe Stress Scale as the "second most stressful life event a person can experience, second only to death of a spouse."

So, when all your well-meaning friends and relatives are telling you that it is time to "get over it," please take that time to instead check in with yourself and think about what you are grieving for. You are not being silly, overly emotional, or pathetic. An enormous part of your identity just got taken away from you, to say nothing of the loss you feel of a former best friend, confidante, and financial partner.

You are not only grieving for the past but also for the future you had thought was pretty much set.

It will be hard for sure. You are probably in a very negative mental space. I know that right after I got divorced, I was frustrated and found myself blaming others or circumstances for my situation. Given this, what to do to get yourself out from under the bed covers every day in the beginning? For me a big part of it was that I did have to take care of my children still. They weren't babies, but they still were not able to fend for themselves. They still had lives that involved school and activities and friends. Added to that was the fact that they were grieving too. I saw it as my job to try and keep as much a sense of "normal" as possible. Kids aside, sitting around in your house may feel like a perfect cocoon, but the longer you sit in that space, the harder it will be to move out of it. Every day, you need to put on something other than yoga pants, slap some makeup on your face, and get out of your house. The expression "fake it 'til you make it" springs to mind. The more you tell your brain that you are a fully functioning and capable human being, the more you will come to believe that yourself. Smiling like a loon at people you pass may seem a little extreme, but it will cause people to smile back at you and that leads to good feelings inside. That's just what you need right now! I know this works because I've experimented a few times while out walking and curious to see what people would do. Some looked surprised but most responded in kind. No one ran away screaming, so give it a go.

One of my clients who was finding it difficult to leave her house told me that she would put on the same pair of elastic-waisted shorts each day. She described them as being the kind that a middle schooler wears for gym and confided in me that a couple of her friends had joked with her about them. I asked her why she was wearing them. We went through various reasons. They were comfortable, handy, and she liked to wear them while walking the dog. Then I asked her how she would feel if she had to meet lots of people on her dog walks wearing these shorts. She told me that she wouldn't want anyone to see her that way. This was her way of hiding. She agreed that they had to go! To make sure they didn't emerge from the bottom of her wardrobe a week later, her homework was to cut them up and throw them away. It sounds drastic, but the next week I heard all about the way she was now feeling wearing clothes that made her feel confident and ready to meet the world.

You can get out and go anywhere. Be around other people. Meet a friend for coffee. Indulge in an afternoon at a museum if you want to be alone. Go and buy a really cute journal and write down everything that you are feeling, no matter how venomous—just don't read it back later.

Gossiping with friends, scaring strangers with your over-friendly smile, filling journals, or manifesting a new man to sweep you off your feet are a few of the baby steps to begin your journey, but they are not all that's around to help you move on from your midlife divorce. In this book, I am going to share with you the seven vital steps I use with my clients that can serve to get you off that couch into a positive mindset and feeling confident and secure permanently.

Something I noticed after my own divorce is that there is no end of people who will want to rehash your marriage and gossip about what your ex is up to now. These are people that you may want to consider spending much less time with.

In fact, the first vital step to moving on after divorce is to stop focusing on what you thought life was going to be for you. Looking back at the past is certain to make sure that you will not see the present and definitely have no chance to look forward. If you are always indulging the need to find out what your ex is up to, then how will you live your own life? Several months after my husband left home and had clearly moved on, it was my fifteen-year-old daughter who pointed out to me that perhaps my wearing my wedding ring was not living in my reality now. (Actually, she said it was "pathetic, Mom" but I got the greater point and she was correct). When I did take it off and leave it off for good, I really did feel an emotional lifting, an actual cut of a physical tie between us, the realization that it was me now, not us.

Financial insecurity after divorce is a real and reasonable fear. Even if we come from a financially stable marriage, often we have no idea how much or how little money we will have when the whole agonizing ordeal is over. As wrong as it seems in this day and age of equality, many of the women I work with see this as their main area of concern. It was certainly something that I couldn't even really think about. Even with the ability to work as a teacher, it looked to me that my future was suddenly on very shaky financial ground. It calls all our basic needs into question. Housing, food, and the ability to look after my children were my main needs.

My reaction was to ignore the problem, and it took me some time to really face this issue. I'm hoping to save you from that mistake here.

After my divorce, I was so excited that I had finally lost the weight I had put on over the years. Boy, did I look great! I believe there is actually a term, the "Divorce Diet." It's amazing what all that stress and anxiety can do to you. It didn't last too long because, in my case, that pendulum swung back the other way really fast! Emotional eating was my way of coping and the reason that everyone kept telling me how amazingly well I was dealing with everything. Little did they know that cookies, wine, and my nights out that didn't end until two a.m. when the kids were with their dad was the real way I was getting by so well. Take it from me: This is not a long-term solution. Vital step number three is to look at what you're doing to make yourself feel better. If, like me, they are actually making things worse, then it's time to replace these coping techniques with something more positive and effective.

After divorce, a whole range of feelings can overwhelm you. They will range from anger to remorse to confusion to profound sadness. Maybe all of them in one day! Your emotions are real and valid. Stuffing them down and soldiering bravely on will only lead to bigger problems down the road. I should know because I'm British! Don't mistake what I'm saying to you here though. I definitely do not want you to retire to the couch with a pint of ice cream or a bottle of wine as a permanent status. Feeling all your emotions means dealing with them. They won't suddenly disappear, but this is the time to get control of them, rather than them having control over you. Step number four will leave you feeling more stable and allow you to let go of deep wounds that are holding you back.

Step number five is a particularly tough one because you need to be willing to move out of your comfort zone and dig deep. It is *so* worth it, and if you commit to changing your life and being ready to love your future, you can't skip this one. It involves looking at what you are saying to and about yourself daily. What do you really believe about yourself in opposition to the reality of who you actually are and how fabulous you can be? If these negative beliefs are false, how come you think them and where did they come from? More importantly perhaps, how can you replace them with the truth?

Divorce brings all sorts of surprises, which include how much it changes relationships. Relationships you took for granted may collapse or end up being the foundation of your support. Whether it be mutual friends, neighbors, or in-laws, keep in mind that those close to you are processing their own feelings and may not be able to be an immediate pillar of support. It is important to recognize and be prepared for this. My family was living 3,000 miles away from me when I got divorced. My large in-law family had been in my life for about twenty years. To find that they were mostly not around anymore, especially in a time of crisis, was very difficult. Losing your social and family connections can end up leaving you feeling isolated and alone. Managing this part of your life is an important part of moving on and is step number six.

Once you have gone through the first six steps, you will be emerging confident and feeling the truth of how fabulous you truly are. This is the time to find out what your goals and passions in life are now. Having spent so many years looking to other people's needs, whether it be the kids or the ex or other friends and family, I have found that the clients I work with have never actually thought about what it is that they love in life. Where is it that they want to go now? This is now your time to set goals and do the things you love to make your heart and soul sing.

Chapter 4
{ "Change" Can Mean "Better" }

"In the process of letting go, you will lose many things from the past, but you will find yourself."
— **Deepak Chopra**

Going into the marriage, we often have an expectation of how everything is going to work out. We think that now life is pretty set in so far as it will be a partnership that carries us through whatever comes along. Of course, everyone has different ideas of what and how much we want that partner to carry of the decision making and the way that we live. However, no one probably goes into their marriage expecting that it isn't going to work out.

When we get married, we have a certain view of the man we are going to share all this with. Sometimes there are doubts in the background that maybe crept up on us before the actual wedding but that were pushed down because we wanted this to work out. It is amazing the capacity we have as humans to look at a situation that, if it were a friend we were advising, we might tell them to think carefully about getting too involved but that we push aside and make excuses for. Sometimes we want something to be a certain way so badly, that wishing, wanting, and believing override common sense, our gut reactions, and basically the truth of a situation. An example of this would be when you are in a relationship where your boyfriend has had many relationships and a couple of marriages already and his story about all of them was that these women were to blame in various ways for how badly they treated him. Then you hear all about his family and how they are all so mean to him that he doesn't have a relationship with them anymore. This should be a huge waving red flag that perhaps all of these other people are not the problem but the one common denominator is him. It is so easy to ignore your gut on this. I know because I went into a long relationship with this very kind of person. Of course, more issues arose, but the deeper into the relationship you get, the more excuses you make because, as you see it, you have invested so much into it already.

Once in the marriage, it is even harder to admit that there are flaws with the man that you have invested so much into. Even if no red flags arose to you before, things like controlling behavior, basic disrespect of your opinions, or outright verbal abuse can creep up on you slowly so that you almost don't notice that they are happening at all.

I know that in my marriage, friends told me later so many things that they noticed my ex said to me that was a put-down when we were together that I had not even acknowledged on a conscious level. Indeed, when I looked back after my divorce, I found things about our life together that I was surprised that I would ever have put up with, that seemed perfectly rational and acceptable at the time. When this is the case, a couple of things can happen. Either the woman realizes that this is happening for some reason and decides that she cannot live like this, and she is the one who initiates the divorce. This can lead to many issues in itself after the fact. Or divorce is brought up by the husband, so it comes as a total shock to the wife and she feels blindsided. Totally unable to process how this could have come about. To her, she had a wonderful marriage.

This is what I hear from so many of the women I speak to. They will tell me of an incident during their marriage where the man was emotionally abusive and controlling. Yet when I point this out to her, she will make excuses for his behavior, even though he has now divorced her and moved on. In fact, I find that so many of us will not only excuse him but will then continue on to take the blame onto herself. We are still trapped in the patterns that we had with our ex-husband even though he has gone.

Added to this is the view that the future that was basically all planned out has now radically changed. You saw yourself working out the financial future, your social interactions, your leisure time, the way that you coped with children as a couple.

Now that has completely changed. All that you can see at the moment is that none of those things are possible on your own.

Of course, this is all going to hit you hard. You are entitled to grieve over this loss of the stable future you thought you were going to have. While doing this, there is the natural tendency to look back on your husband and the life you had together through rather rose-tinted glasses. A big factor in being able to move on from this spot, however, is to look at what your marriage really was in realistic terms. No one has a perfect relationship. We are all human, but by not focusing on the idealized version of your story, it may help to see why this was inevitable and how you can find the better version of yourself now that you are not in this relationship anymore.

In order to do this, there are some important questions to ask yourself. You can jot them down and then take some time to think about each one and journal your thoughts. Try to be honest about the way that you are feeling now, without excuses and without assigning blame to anyone in particular. Look at it with curiosity not judgement as much as you are able to.

- What would you say were the top three emotions that hit you the hardest during the divorce?
- What are the top three emotions now?
- If they have changed, why do you think that is?
- What did you expect your life would be like as a married woman?
- Did your expectations come true?
- What was the difference, and why was that?

- Did your ex-husband always treat your opinions with respect?

- When something didn't go the way you wanted it when you were married, who was it that usually took the blame?

- During your marriage, how did you feel about yourself in regard to:
  o Intelligence?
  o Ability to make good decisions alone?
  o Confidence?
  o Looks?

- Did you have your own friends outside of being a couple?

- What were you most worried about as you started the divorce process?

- What has been the best thing to come out of your divorce for you?

As mentioned earlier, it can be very hard to break the patterns of behavior we had with our ex-husbands even though we aren't married to them anymore. We find that we lose who we are in marriage. Our identity becomes tied to our husband or children early on, and so when the marriage ends and these roles are lost or diminished, we can feel unsure of who we really are. So, we keep on playing the role that we had before because we feel that that is the person we have to be. If you are not able to move away from thinking of yourself in these terms, then it will be extremely difficult to move on and thrive as an individual. You will feel tied to your ex-husband and be constantly be looking back on the life that you think you should be living.

After I became divorced, my ex-husband continued to be very critical of basically every decision that I made about my life or about the children. He would regularly send me incredibly long emails outlining something I had done and providing his list of how and why I was wrong and misguided. They were very upsetting to read. I would be angry and anxious and back to the conflict in the divorce all over again. In my opinion, they were unfair, did not consider relevant facts, and in some cases, were just mean.

But I read them all to the end. I shared with my friends the latest stuff he was saying about me. "Can you believe this?" I would say. In fact, they would cause me to stew and basically ruin my day. So later, I would sit down and write a reply going point by point, defending myself, outlining my reasons, or how he was wrong and send them back to him. After this had gone on for a period of some months, a friend said to me, "Why don't you just ignore them?"

It was so obvious, but I never saw it for myself. Why did I care what he thought anymore? Why did it matter if what I did upset him? Why was I allowing him to keep this negative connection? The reason was of course that I had felt that I really needed to prove to him that I was capable of living my life and making decisions all by myself.

So, I stopped reading any of these types of emails from him. I had to keep connected because it may relate to the children, but otherwise I totally ignored them. Then they just stopped coming. I felt calmer, relieved, and I had an overwhelming sense that I was in control of my life. It was so liberating to realize that I didn't care what he thought or told other people about me. If they knew me, they could judge for themselves. If they didn't know me, it wasn't important. That moment, when I let go of worrying or caring about what he thought of my life, was a giant leap forward for me.

It is really all about changing your reaction, rather than expecting the behavior of your ex to change. You know logically that we have zero control over the way other people behave. No matter how much we will someone to do the right thing, as we see it, or to suddenly start to live a different way, it is not going to happen unless they want to. So the easier path and the one that will help you to get results for your own life is to simply change the way that you react to their behavior if it is affecting you.

Staying connected in whatever way it happens is a certain way to stop us living in the present moment or moving on as a single woman. Sometimes, it isn't only the behavior of the ex that is doing this. We can justify anything to ourselves to keep this close connection. Even though being stuck in this way is very uncomfortable and makes us feel sad or angry, these emotions are protecting us from what we unconsciously really fear which is to let go and launch into our new reality after the divorce. Of course, if there are children involved, there is going to be a need for contact and communication about them. For their sake, it is very important to make this a civil as possible. However, this does not mean that you not respect the new lives and boundaries of the ex. I had a client who was holding on to a key from her ex's house because she would need to go in there on occasion to pick up things that her child had left.

Now, in actual fact, none of these things were that vital and could have been picked up on the next visit or dropped off by the father. She was using the key to go in the home and look around to see what was going on in the ex's life now. When I asked her why, she said that she just wanted to know what he was doing.

"Ok," I said. "What have you found out that has made you feel happy or good about yourself?"

Well, there was nothing to make her feel that way, but a couple of things that made her feel quite the opposite. So, we agreed that the key was not serving a positive purpose for her, and she gave it to her child to give back to his father. She said that she actually felt a sense of relief that she didn't have to go in there anymore. This may seem an extreme case, but if you consider how many of us would regularly look at a Facebook page or ask friends about the lives of our exes, then you can see that you are getting pretty much the same result. There is no upside to this hanging on.

You may feel that you have cut the cord to your ex-husband by the very fact that you are now divorced. In reality, it is not always the case. The emotional bonds that still keep us attached, even the negative ones, are extremely hard to get rid of. This is in part because we don't even realize that they are still there. This is our uncomfortable comfort zone. Our very identity is still wrapped up in this attachment and that is why it is so difficult to let go of. Who will we be now without it?

Letting go of this death grip on the past and recognizing that the fear is what is keeping you stuck in this place is a very large step towards finding out who you are now and how much you are capable of achieving. If you are able to let go of relying on your ex and your past marriage to give yourself your sense of who you are, if you are able to let go of the idea of the life that you thought you would be living as part of a couple, if you can do this part of the equation, then the older "when I was married" view of what your future was going to be will also be easier to let go of. It will be easier to see that there are different possibilities for you now, perhaps even better possibilities because this future will be one that you are more in control of. A fun activity is to sit down a write out a bucket list for yourself. Put anything on that list whether you think it is possible or not. It can range from taking a cruise to the Mediterranean, to learning to tango, to meditating for five minutes per day. You can create your own list and keep it posted somewhere handy. Having small items that you can tick off easily is a great way to reconnect with who you are and begin seeing yourself as separate from your ex. It's also great for building confidence in your abilities and taking care of yourself. If you need support, you could find a friend to do it with you or get a coach to help with encouragement, accountability, and to celebrate your successes.

Here's the thing about life. It will keep going forward whether you want it to or not. You can stay locked in your past or step out of your fear to push forward into the unknown. No matter how badly you are feeling right now, it is vitally important to remember that this is always your choice. Now more than ever.

Chapter 5
{ Facing Financial Realities }

"When you are grateful- when you can see what you
have- you unlock blessings to flow in your life."
– Suze Orman

ociology and law professor and author Lenore Weitzman
believes that women are more likely to face damaging
financial consequences and a diminished standard of living than
men. Getting divorced in midlife is a very different experience
for a woman than for her spouse. Her studies found that after a
divorce, a woman experiences a seventy-three percent reduction
in standard of living while a man's standard of living is enhanced
by forty-two percent.

That's a pretty daunting statistic, especially in this day and age when we like to think that women's equality has come so far. But the truth of the matter is that many women who are getting divorced in midlife have either put their own careers on hold at some point to look after children or stayed home completely. Regardless of their job status, when we go from a household that has an adequate income or two incomes to two separate households, there is naturally going to be a drop in the standard of living.

So, fear about our financial future is a very reasonable and real consequence of getting divorced for most. Even if we come from a financially stable marriage, often we have no idea how much or how little money we will have when the whole agonizing ordeal is over. There are so many factors determining alimony. It can vary from state to state and circumstances of the marriage.

An article in Forbes magazine backs up the belief that women who divorce in midlife are more likely to have a difficult time when dealing with finances in their new life. This is especially true for those who stayed home to be with children. Add to this the sad fact that even today, in general men tend to have higher incomes and a more consistent work history. That often means that once the family finances are split, it is easier for men to get back into the swing of financial stability. The longer the marriage and the older the spouses, the harder this can be for the woman to find that security.

So, what are you to do if you are dreading the future and wondering what you will do about feeling financially stable? If you do not take control of your finances as soon as possible, then the problem will compound. You will feel a lack of control, not know what you can and should spend, and even wonder about whether you can keep a roof over your head. Your stress, fear, and anxiety will soar. Looking after your financial health and fully knowing your situation, no matter the state of it, will give you that feeling of control that you need. Feeling in control of a situation will lessen your stress. You will be able to budget adequately and know what you need to do in order to meet your current and future needs, eliminating the fear that you might have about how you are going to manage. Instead of ignoring it or constantly bemoaning the fact that it isn't fair, now is the time to act. If you face the fear and make the right preparations, whatever the position you are starting from, you can overcome and move on with confidence.

If you are worried that you aren't able to look at your situation by yourself, it is worth finding a professional to help you. Whether it is an accountant or a financial advisor, having a person who is not emotionally involved in your situation can really help you to get a realistic perspective on your position.

One of my clients became divorced after thirty-three years of marriage. Her husband had asked her to retire from her teaching job of many years a year previously so that they could travel and move to a warmer climate. She was no longer earning any money of her own. They had a couple of properties and had planned to retire to a warmer state by the end of the next year. Then, he told her that he had filed for divorce. She was left devastated. As she told me, he had always looked after that whole side of things, and she didn't feel like she had the financial knowledge to realize that she should have gone through a lawyer and not mediation. She was left in a rather bad financial situation. However, she found a financial planner to help her sort through her remaining assets. On her advice she went back to work and sold her house. She was then able to buy a more manageable home and live comfortably. This was not the way that she had expected to live these next years of her life, but she faced the reality of the situation. Once she was able to see a path to moving forward, it lifted a huge burden and things progressed in a much smoother manner. She felt more in control of her life and proud that she had delved into something that terrified her so much. She told me that she had the first decent night's sleep in a long time after her first consultation.

Whether you decide to use a professional to help you or you are able to do this on your own, the first thing that you will need to do is look at your post-divorce assets. Make sure you know everything about your new financial situation. How much equity do you have in your home? How much do you have in savings? How much do you have in any retirement accounts? How much in the bank? Do you have significant debt? Write it all down so that you can see exactly what your situation is. After that, make a list of the expenses that you have on a monthly basis. Make sure that you include as much detail in there as possible, not only major items like mortgages and utilities but also don't forget little details like vet bills, hair styling for the family, insurance, any activities that your children take on a regular basis that need to be paid for. The next step is to then write down all the money that is coming into the house monthly. If there is a large deficit between spending and income, then it is time to take a hard look at what can be cut. Living on a budget is not sexy or fun by any means. However, it will give you the sense of stability that you are looking for. It will lessen the nasty surprise that can crop up at the end of every month. Build in savings as a part of the budget as much as you can. That way you feel better about the future and get to use it for the more fun aspects of life (like vacations!) or have it available for the inevitable hiccups in life, like a car breakdown.

One of my many mistakes after my divorce was that I spent huge amount of money on my children that I possibly could have saved. I helped my older children out with buying cars, rent, and other expenses that could have been avoided—the kids could have even saved and taken responsibility for them! This has been a theme that I have heard from many of my clients. As mothers, we feel responsible for our kids, and we want to do everything for them. When the father has decided that he isn't going to help out in these areas, it is often the case that we overcompensate. If that is possible in your budget and you are still able to save for the future, then by all means do as much for them as you like, but if helping them out is causing your hardship, then sometimes you will need to take a hard look at this situation and let your kids know the reality of the situation. You are not being selfish, and it doesn't mean you love them less.

Depending on what you have been doing during the marriage, you may need to think about finding a better source of income. If you have been staying home raising the family, this can be scary. Many of the women that I talk to procrastinate at taking this step, not because they don't want to work but because they feel that they are not able to do anything. Finding the confidence in yourself is ninety percent of the battle in this area. I have found that women have far more skills than they ever give themselves credit for at the end of their divorces. One thing that you can do is reach out to anyone that you think works in an industry that you are interested in. Asking someone to have a cup of coffee is casual and requires no commitment, so you won't have to feel like you are pressuring them. Most people are really happy to help out in any case. They can give you tips about what employers may be looking for or even give you leads to contact in your area. Sometimes you can start off by working part time, as a substitute teacher for example. You gain recent experience and are positioned for any openings that come up. The most important thing is to be open to all opportunities. Do not think that no one will want you and shy away. Say yes to everything and see what comes your way.

One client I worked with had a passion for interior design. She hadn't had any formal training but had always found people raving about whatever she did in her home and that of friends she had helped out. When a realtor she knew suggested that she contact a local woman who did staging to see if she could do work with her, her first reaction was to say no. This was because she felt that she was not good enough to work with this other professional woman. What she was not thinking about was that the realtor was putting her reputation on the line by introducing them, so obviously she thought that there was a good shot at them working together. The stager was happy to meet and take a look at her designs. The only thing holding back the client was her own fear. Always look at the worst case and the best case if you are unsure what to do. The worst case was that they had coffee and the stager decided that she wasn't ready to work together. Nothing lost. The best case was that the stager looked at her designs and was delighted and they started working together and my client was able to make money in a job that she loved.

Meanwhile, she did some work for friends and then used the photographs from that to add to her portfolio. She went to networking events where she met other realtors and told them what she was doing. Taking that first step out of your comfort zone can be incredibly scary but can really pay back in major ways.

Whether you are working or not, if you are receiving some kind of support from your ex-husband, not understanding the tax implications can really trip you up! Taxes after divorce can get very complicated. One rule of thumb is that the person receiving alimony has to pay taxes on that money. The one paying alimony gets a tax deduction. Child support, however, is not taxed on the person receiving it. Taxes have become a very specialized and complicated part of any divorce settlement, so talk to an expert about that if you have any doubts or questions. I can personally tell you that I got blindsided by this one. I had not known that you are supposed to pay taxes on your alimony, and I was slapped with a $20,000 bill the first April after my divorce! If you do not know that this is coming and didn't pay estimated taxes or put money aside, I can tell you that it is very difficult to suddenly come up with the money. Many of the women I have spoken to have also found this out the hard was also.

There are so many areas that need to be addressed after you get divorced, but finances are probably the one area that I hear about the most as the biggest fear when I talk to women. It is truly the uncertainty of the situation that seems to cause the most angst and be the main reason that keeps them up at night. By taking some of the steps above, you will be able to alleviate some of that uncertainty. If you face the fear and make the right preparations, whatever the position you are starting from, you can overcome and move on with confidence.

{

Chapter 6
Eliminating
Destructive Habits

}

"You cannot find peace by avoiding life."
– Virginia Woolf

When exposed to very stressful situations, human beings react in many different ways in order to cope and process with the feelings that they need to deal with. Divorce is so incredibly stressful and brings up so many different emotions that it can cause us to look for all kinds of different ways to make us feel better. When faced with an overwhelm of emotions or fear, then an escape is just what we need. In my own experience and from talking to many women who have gone through this process, I have found that not too many of us come out of this without some kind of coping strategy. For the most part, they aren't the best things for us. You may find yourself acting out in destructive and uncharacteristic ways. When feeling down, you can experience intrusive thoughts and an overwhelming sense of hopelessness. It is only natural then to indulge ourselves in ways that bolster our mood, even if for a short time. However, recognizing these behaviors is a vital step to guarding against them. It is important to understand that the short term boost you get from this is actually working against your long-term ability to heal and move on in a positive way.

Emotional eating was for me was, perhaps, the biggest coping strategy that I employed. It had always been hanging around as my go-to stress reducer, something that had helped me through difficult issues in my younger life. As I got older and more settled, I had thought that it was more under control, but the divorce and tailspin that resulted from that threw me right back into this habit with a vengeance. From the sudden weight loss when I first found out I was getting a divorce, I swung around and began to steadily put on weight over the course of the next few years. I knew it was happening. When something happened with one of my kids or I had some negative interaction with my ex, I would find myself by the cookie jar telling myself that just this once was ok and I could deal with it later. But you know that the only thing that actually happens later is the regret and self-loathing that goes along with your "weakness" and not being in control of yourself, all those nasty things you say in your head and the things that pop into your mind when you look in the mirror. So of course, when you are feeling so low and rotten about yourself, the natural pick me up is... yes, another snack to make yourself feel better, on and on in this endless spiral. Yet the issues that are driving you to this do not go away and now you feel even worse about yourself.

If you have this issue, the first thing you need to do is to stop beating yourself up about it! Willpower and being "weak" is not your problem. There are many ways to start to be mindful of what you are eating and when, and more importantly why, In fact, there are whole books on this very topic. That is the first thing you need to address, not start that crash diet that will not work or last more than a few days before you give up in a flurry of tears and binge eating. A tip to start you off and one of the first things that I use when I work with clients is to look at the times and things you are eating from a standpoint of curiosity, not judgement. Whenever you feel the need to go to that snack place, firstly see if there is anything else that you could do to distract yourself for a few minutes. Often cravings will pass if you get involved in something else. Have a cup of herbal tea or a warm shower or take the dog out, as examples. If that isn't working for you, ok, then without self judgement, answer a few questions of yourself.

- What time of day is it?
- What emotion do you feel the strongest right now?
- Did you try anything first to distract you?
- What was I thinking or doing right before I wanted to snack?
- How hungry do I really feel on a scale of 1-10?
- Is there anything I am trying to avoid doing?

If you still want the snack, go ahead because holding back will make you eat more anyway very soon. However, write down what emotions you are feeling five and ten minutes after you have eaten.

After a few days, you should start to see a pattern emerging that can help you to head off these triggers before they cause you to snack.

If it has become a habit to have a calming glass of wine, or two, or more in the evening, this can add to the food that you are eating. Alcohol leads to lowering our boundaries, and so a little pint of ice cream doesn't seem that bad after all. Until the next day. Whether it causes you to eat more or not, the evening glass of wine can easily dissolve in to quite a bad habit if you don't keep an eye on it. When you think that you are using alcohol as a way to relax on a regular basis, you need to realize that what you are really doing is using it to numb out the things that you don't want to deal with. This is a much bigger problem in the end and can lead to a place where more serious professional help is needed. If you aren't sure if it is a problem that is getting out of control to the point that it affects your regular daily functioning, start keeping an honest record of what and how much you drink daily and reach out for help from someone you trust.

Sometimes the partying is of a more social nature. I know that when I got divorced and discovered new friends who were also newly divorced, going out and having fun was high on our list of priorities. We had been home looking after children and working for years, and now suddenly, here was the opportunity to not have to rush home to the family. We weren't accountable to someone else anymore, and it was time to let loose! While incredibly fun at the time, however, too much of this good thing for too long will have consequences.

My client, Rhonda, was definitely drinking and partying more than was healthy. It was beginning to impact her work, her relationship with her children, and her health. It was also leading her to make poor decisions in other areas of her life, such as relationships. Meeting men while out with friends was leading to a lot of dates and then a lot of disappointments once she got to know them a little better. She began to think that she was the problem and that she would never have another serious relationship again. Once we were able to help her make the shift from feelings to rational thinking about what she really wanted and what she was trying to avoid, then she was able to stop the emotional tailspin. She was still experiencing some of those feelings, but they were not controlling her anymore. She stopped going out three nights every week and instead found more constructive ways to connect with friends. She started to concentrate on her goals for the new life she wanted to live. She joined a gym and actually lost a significant amount of weight. Her relationship with her children improved, and through all this, her self-esteem rose, prompting new positive goals and actions. She found that she was not interested in the same type of controlling romantic relationships that she had before.

The temptation to want to go out and buy lots of new things can also be a big problem as a way to fill that need to feel better about yourself. It follows the same exhilaration, realization, and regret pattern as the emotional eating habit. At least with the shopping, you can return the items if you want to do that. The problem that you fall into here is that it ties in to financial fears and fears about how you are going to manage your future. If this is a huge problem for you, then taking such measures as cutting up credit cards or freezing them in a block of ice in the freezer is really not too drastic. There is something about the handing over of actual money that reminds us more clearly of how much something is actually costing us. If boredom or needing to distract yourself when your children are at their father's house is what is leading you to go to the mall, then plan activities that you can do at those times before they come up. That way you already have something to do.

It can be very painful to face the emotions these behaviors mask. That is why it is often necessary to find help to support you with this. Indeed, initially a large part of what I do with my clients deals with their coping strategies that have been compounding the problems and fears that they are facing. A way of looking at this is that it is necessary to make the shift from feeling to thinking when you are finding that you are using bad habits as a form of escapism. By this I mean being acutely aware of what it is that you are doing, what it is costing you, what is triggering you. Then looking at how you would rather be feeling and rationally thinking about ways to get you there.

With any of these habits, or others that I haven't touched on here, there are solutions to combat them. If this was not your regular behavior before your divorce or even if it was something that you employed at times of extreme stress, then there were probably things that you liked to do before that did not have these negative consequences. Think about any of the good habits you may have lost since you got divorced. Even if you feel that your life revolved around taking care of the family and now that is taking up so much less time, sit down and make a list of things that you would like to do. This is now your time to do things for yourself.

I found that after fifteen straight years of feeling that I was never alone in my house, those first weekends when my children went to their father's were incredibly strange. Which, in part, accounted for my falling into some of the habits listed above, I started out by painting nearly every room in my house because that is something that I love to do. It also had the added benefit of making it my own new space. Then I moved on to buying canvases from the local craft store and playing around on them. For sure there are no great works of art with my name on out there, but I did really enjoy the activity, and it was really calming to me as well as, to be honest, the distraction that I sometimes needed from the stresses that I was facing at the time. I came to really value the alone time that I had every other weekend and stopped feeling the need to fill it with doing things for other people (even those that I loved) or actively looking like I was having "a good time."

You can make yourself a list of the things that you enjoy doing and that help you to feel happy and relaxed. It really doesn't matter what they are, and they don't have to cost money. They can range from exercise to hobbies like gardening or painting, to meditation or healthy cooking. It doesn't matter, but what does matter is that these healthier habits can replace the destructive ones and boost your energy and self-esteem.

Chapter 7
Reframe Emotions

"The weak can never forgive.
Forgiveness is the attribute of the strong."
– Mahatma Gandhi

There are so many emotions battling within you after the end of your relationship.

I have heard them all in varying degrees and mixed together in different ways from my clients. Boiled down, the main ones are anger, guilt, sadness, and confusion. However, there is a generous sprinkling of resentment and bitterness thrown in there, too.

What they do have in common, whatever degree you have them to, or whatever mixture you are dealing with is that they are keeping you trapped in chronic pain and a sense of numbness that is not allowing you to move on with the rest of your life.

When your energy is totally focused on these negative emotions, it blinds you to the possibilities of your present and future, and it is a sure-fire way to stay connected to the past.

Sometimes these emotions are almost the only thing that gets us up in the morning. They fuel the energy that we have to get through the day. It is all too easy to relive the worst things we feel have been done to us over and over again in order to fuel that negative emotion. Why do we do this? That anger, or sadness, or guilt, becomes a place that makes it easy to explain why things are not going the way we think they should. These totally uncomfortable and ugly emotions become our comfort zone, a security blanket that we are unwilling to let go of even though it is an awful place to be. They become our way of protecting us from something else that we think will be much worse. Usually that is the fear of what will happen next. This is what holds women back from breaking out and moving on.

"Holding onto anger is like drinking poison and expecting the other person to die." This quote has been attributed to various people, but it doesn't matter who said it first; the principal is what matters.

When you are letting yourself go through these negative emotions every day, the only person that is feeling the pain is you. You may also be affecting the loved ones around you, like your children or your coworkers, because it is impossible to be our best selves in this state.

Not only may you be a permanent grouch to be around in this state, but it is affecting your health in very negative ways.

You will have lack of sleep and lots of little aches and pains. It causes us to be careless, and accidents happen. If it goes on long enough, it can even cause serious illnesses to manifest.

Bad decisions all come from being in a negative state. When you make these, it only serves to justify your view of yourself as someone who is not able to make any decisions at all.

It would be relatively easy to see why women feel angry when the marriage ends because the spouse has cheated or left them suddenly in a difficult situation. Every time something occurs that is difficult to deal with, the anger at being left alone with it can surge up all over again. A single woman now has to deal with all kinds of things that were not solely on her plate before. Parenting can become much more of a burden when you are the one making all the decisions or even just logistically by getting children from one activity to another. Financial decisions or household tasks take on a bigger stress level when they have to be tackled alone. All of this can trigger an angry response at the spouse who is no longer available to help out and has left you to do this while seemingly going off without any responsibilities.

For many of my clients, a further trigger is the ex-husband's new relationship. From her perspective, the two are now living an easier, more carefree, and often more financially stable life than the ex-wife is living.

My client Sally came to me particularly angry because she felt that she had been left with the burden of dealing with all the things around the house and large property that had to be looked after. She was the one who had to now keep track of and pay the bills, clean out the garage, paint the house, and manage all the little daily tasks that were needed to maintain a home. She felt that her ex-husband was now off somewhere with no responsibilities and able to enjoy life, while she was left to do all the hard work.

When we went through the exercises to see what was really coming up for her, she discovered that looking back, she had done all those things when she was married while he had spent time on things that he wanted to do for himself. In hindsight, she realized that not only was she doing it all anyway, but she had always had to listen his opinion about how things should be done as well as his criticisms. In regard to doing the tasks, nothing had actually changed for her. However, now she was in charge of how and what she did. She came to realize that she was a much stronger person than she had thought initially.

When dealing with anger, however, I have found that many women are surprised to realize that it is directed not only at their ex-husband but at themselves as well. They think that they should have done more to keep their husband happy or engaged in the marriage. If only they had been that "better" woman, then none of this would have happened in the first place. This can come from various places. If you were always the one to blame when things went wrong in the relationship by default, then it is difficult to let go of that type of thinking about yourself. Often, I have heard that the man has told the wife outright that this is totally her fault because of her shortcomings. Sometimes the anger can come because you cannot believe that you could have let yourself get put into such a position to allow the behavior of your ex in the first place. Again, you are blaming yourself entirely. It is important to understand that you are never in the position to be responsible for someone else's happiness or feeling of self-worth. That is something that comes from within. After spending years of feeling like you were walking on eggshells for fear of upsetting your ex or spending so much time pandering to his wants and needs at the expense of your own, it is time to fully understand that no matter how much attention or cheerleading you give someone else; if they do not treat you well or appreciate their life, it is not because of your lack.

Along with the anger comes guilt and often the feeling of failure. This personal responsibility for things not working out as they "should."

Then what can you do about it? At some point, you have to reach out and consciously begin to manage your emotions. This will become easier to do as you begin to understand how this hangover from your divorce starts, what keeps it in place, what yours looks like, what it's protecting you from, and how you can release it.

Moving from just experiencing these emotions to rationally thinking about your situation is the way to stop the emotional tailspin that you have got yourself into. If you can think about something, you can put it outside of yourself. The emotions aren't going to just disappear, but they don't have the control over you that they did.

Hard as it is going to be, there are things you can do to help relieve these emotions. You need to be open to the various possibilities for healing, which may take place in the form of therapy, spiritual assistance, support groups, books, or a coach. Whatever you do, it is most important that you open yourself up to the necessary process for healing your heart.

You will need to care for yourself. Not just physically but also emotionally and spiritually. In doing so, you can feel the pain, yes, but then find it easier to release it. Give yourself permission to grieve all those losses that came from the divorce. They are real, but in acknowledging them, you can then be open and excited by the new possibilities ahead for you. Most importantly, you need to resist the urge for revenge. It rarely turns out the way you think it will and will only serve to prolong the negative feelings that are making you feel so badly. As a partner to this, being able to forgive is extremely important.

Forgiveness is possibly the hardest yet the most effective thing that anyone can do in order to move on to a new and happy life. And there is possibly a long list of those that may need your forgiveness. The most prominent of those being your ex-spouse, the new woman in his life, and don't forget yourself. I can almost hear you screaming at me from wherever you are reading this book. I know. How can I suggest such a thing? Understand that this is not to "let him off the hook" for some awful thing that he did to you, even may be continuing to do to you… This is to let you off the hook of carrying the burden of swirling in these nasty feelings that are keeping you stuck in your track, unable to move forward and experience the joy that you deserve.

When you can forgive someone else, it's about helping you move on rather than letting them get away with something. Let's face it—you cannot go back and change the past. You cannot control the way that your ex thinks or behaves. Your control is in the way that you react and behave. How much power will you feel when you decide to move away from this negative attachment and start to live your best life? One powerful way to help you do this is to rewrite the key aspects of your story from a more balanced, empathetic place. This is a place that makes you less of a victim, less devastated, and it can reduce the anger and bitterness that go along with that.

My ex already knew his now wife long before I was aware I was getting a divorce. A year after, they were married and living pretty much right around the corner. This last year, I joined a small Pilates class that only takes twelve clients at a time. One day, I went in, and it was quite a shock to me as I signed in to see her name above mine. I have to admit, I did have a moment of panic. This was a very small setting. All my insecurities came swirling up. Did she look better than me in workout clothes? Would I be all sweaty? What if she could do a longer plank than I could?

I asked myself why I was getting so worked up about it. I think I was looking at the injustice side of it… as I saw it, of course. Shouldn't all these ladies she's chatting to know that she was a part of blowing up my life? Shouldn't they know that she left her kids in another state for a man? Here she is with no need for a job and vacations and a second house… Ok, I was getting out of control for sure! Did I want her to walk around with a big scarlet sign on her? (Well, maybe a little part of me. I am human.) So, I decided to turn around my thinking. It was time for me to reframe this situation and look at reality: who I want to be, how I want to feel and behave. Yes, she was a part of changing my life. However, I had unknowingly been incredibly unhappy in that life I was living. It was even making me physically ill. That relationship was not good for either of us.

Since the end of my marriage, I have changed many of my thought patterns.

I have become more spiritual and definitely believe in things that I had previously thought were just for those loony ladies in the wool socks and sandals.

I have explored my limiting beliefs and found my power.

I have control over my own life.

I am living my dream and passion (that I didn't even know I had) of running my own business helping other women find their power, self-worth, and control. Through that I am travelling more. I meet extraordinary people and get to listen to life changing ideas. I love my life now. Wow! I should go over there and hug her! Of course, I didn't do that. Instead I walked into the studio with a smile on my face and lay down on the reformer a couple of feet away from her. An uneventful class was had by all.

That evening at dinner, I said I had been to Pilates and my daughter shared that her stepmother also went that day. "Oh no, were you there together?" she asked. When I said yes, the kids laughed and asked me if I was going to stop the class in case I bumped into her again. I told them no because I enjoyed the class, and who was there was not important to me. That was when I realized that I had not only learned a very powerful lesson myself, but that I was able to pass something important on to my children.

By letting go of my anger at her—and believe me, I had been extremely angry at her at one point in my life—I was allowing myself to live the life I wanted.

Being angry and frustrated and indignant would have caused me to leave and stop doing something I enjoyed. It would have ruined my whole day as I stewed over it. It would have caused me to spread the "poison" as I told my friends that *she* had been in my class and I had to leave (resenting her more, even though that would have been my choice). There was far more benefit to me to let it go rather than hang on to those negative feelings. They would have hurt no one but myself and possibly my children.

By being conscious of the emotions that are sending you into a tailspin, you can start to get a handle on how to reframe them to allow you to live a calmer, less stressful, and happier life. Think about what is triggering each one. What purpose is it serving for you? Is there something that it is protecting you from that perhaps you need to face up to? If you can step out of that uncomfortable comfort zone and face those fears, it is usually the case that anticipation is far worse than the reality of the situation.

Chapter 8
Silence the Inner Critic!

"Our lives are stories we tell ourselves."
– Nancy Mairs.

There is a little voice in your head that pretends to be all about helping you and protecting you and being the one who tells you the way it is. However, that little voice is actually feeding you a line of total B.S. for the most part!

We say things to ourselves that we would never dream of saying to another person... not out loud, at least! I bet that you know exactly what I'm talking about. She sneaks up on you when you least expect it. Mine was particularly active when I looked in the mirror. She loved to emphasize every flaw that I thought I might have. Strangely, she was silent in her opinions of my better qualities—I never once heard her point out my particularly lovely shoulders, for example. She starts to chatter whenever there are choices to be made or you consider breaking out of your comfort zone. Your inner critic really loves the comfort zone. See if any of the following sound familiar to you:

- I don't make good decisions
- I look too fat/thin/ugly/old/dowdy/wrinkly/whatever
- I can't possibly succeed at that
- I always fail
- Nobody could love me
- I can't do it
- I can't make any money on my own
- I can't have a life on my own
- I never follow through
- I'm not good enough
- Other people can do it better than me
- They will judge me/ the way I look/the things I say
- I can't change

If they do sound familiar, then you know exactly what I am talking about.

The problem with this kind of negative self-talk is that it isn't some kind of tough self-love that will motivate you to do better or push through the hard times. It is actually having the very opposite effect. The more that we say them to ourselves, the more we believe that this is the truth of who we are. Often that carries over into the way that we believe other people see us and finally ending up as the way that we believe that we deserve to be treated.

That is where the problems that we may have noticed in any of our relationships can arise from. If you are having problems looking at yourself as someone who should be treated well or taken seriously, then it is easy to defer to someone else, allow them to treat us badly, and slowly lower boundaries to the point that we feel like there is no control over our own lives. Then along comes the divorce, and now you are out on your own. How can you possibly believe that you will be able to survive never mind thrive? You don't trust your own judgement or your ability to push past challenges at all.

When boundaries are lowered, they tend to be lowered in every aspect of your life: your relationships at work, with friends, with children and romantic ones too. As a result, it is difficult to say "no" to anything you are asked, even if it isn't something you want to do or have time for. Life becomes a long journey where we become uncomfortable in order to make someone else comfortable. This is not ok. So many women believe that it is selfish to turn down others' requests to allow ourselves to be happy. Unfortunately, the fact is that if we feel unhappy, stressed, and bad-tempered, we can't do such a great job of looking after other needs anyway. An interesting way of looking at a situation if you aren't sure is that every time you say "yes" to someone else, you may be saying "no" to something for yourself. If that is true, then maybe politely decline.

All of these negative things that we believe to be true about ourselves are actually ideas and beliefs that have been put into our heads by other people from the time that we were toddling around as the impressionable little sponges that we were as children. They have been reinforced by our exes to a greater or lesser extent, and they have been repeated by us to ourselves enough so that we now think that this is the absolute truth of who we are.

So now, whenever the need arises to face a challenge or improve our lives or speak up at work, these beliefs pop up to shoot us down and keep us in the place we *think* we belong.

If your belief is that you can't follow through on something, then the chances are that you will never follow through on something. If your belief is that no one wants to hear your opinion about things in meetings, then they will probably never hear from you in meetings. Therefore, you get to prove these beliefs correct and stop any progress for yourself.

What if you decided not to listen to the voice? What if you swallowed that fear for once and took the leap to speak up in a meeting at work? Worst case, people ignore you and get on with their day. Nothing has changed. Best case, the boss pulls you aside and says he was really impressed by your innovation and out-of-the-box thinking. Something will most definitely change. Maybe that belief was wrong. Maybe you do have things to contribute that people want to hear. Maybe you can step up and fight for that promotion that is up for grabs.

How will it feel to step into the real you? How will it feel to lean in to your full potential? How will it feel to take control over your life?

This is a good time to start to work on building up your personal power. Once you look closely, you will realize that you are powerful. The problem is that you don't recognize it in yourself yet. This is mainly because you are allowing the past hurts and what you are saying to yourself to hold you back. If you are honest with yourself about what you really want, then it will be easier to move towards it. You will also need to be very honest about the excuses you are using to protect yourself from taking that next step. No judgement from me! They might be excellent reasons, but that doesn't change the fact that they are keeping you fixed in the place you are in now. Remember what you do have now. Focus on that. Once you have the hang of this, then ask yourself where you would most like to create something better in your life to start with. However, be aware that this may change the idea of who you are. You are going to move towards your future self now. In that case, what is the risk to you in letting go of this "old" you? Think about the new perspective and attitude you will need to adopt in order to be this brand-new, powerful you.

I have spoken to many women who tell me that they know they are really smart and capable. Yet everything about the way that they behave shows that they believe the complete opposite. It sounds strange that this could be the case, but the problem here is that there is a huge gap between knowing a fact and believing it.

Carrie is an amazing woman who was a breadwinner wife, mother, nurse, and managed to get two degrees at the same time as accomplishing all these other awesome tasks. Yet in our conversations, she expressed that she couldn't possibly speak up in meetings at work because people would judge her opinions and find them silly and unhelpful. She had no sense of the incredible woman she actually was. Come to find that she had been told by members of her family and by her ex that she wasn't smart and didn't ever know what she was talking about. As a consequence of that, this became her story of who she is. She believed that she was really a huge fraud and was just waiting to be found out and fired. When we looked at the actual fact of her very real accomplishments (and there were many more than I listed here) against the beliefs that she had got from what others had said to her, she saw that it really made no sense for her to feel that way.

She went to the next meeting took a deep breath and said what she was thinking. The world did not cave in on her. No one laughed or pointed. Heads were nodded in agreement. She felt empowered and in control. Suddenly, she had started to tell herself another story about who she was.

These negative beliefs about yourself can be projected out and without conscious thought, they can be picked up by others who will treat you this way too. That is why jumping into a new relationship right after the divorce can often leave you feeling that you are right back in the same kind of relationship that you had with your husband. Women complain that men are all the same or that they attract all the "losers" that are out there. That is because unless you can clear this negative story that you have about yourself and instead project confidence in the way that you deserve to be treated, that same kind of person, with all his own issues and flaws, is always going to be attracted to you. You may see it, but with your lowered boundaries, you will either ignore it or more likely make excuses for why he is behaving this way. You may also quietly tell yourself that this is all you deserve anyway. I can speak to this from experience. After my divorce, I got into a very serious relationship with someone who I thought was so different from my ex that this had to work out. This was a relationship that lasted on and off for about four years. I can tell you that two weeks in, I was questioning things about him. I know for a fact that if he had been going out with one of my friends, I would have told her to end it and block all contact. But I didn't. I made excuses. I allowed myself to be manipulated. I allowed myself to make decisions that my gut was screaming at me not to. In the end, he turned out to have very similar traits to my ex-husband, just in a different package. I ended it and was drawn back in several times until the final straw was that he was cheating on me. When I found that out, I can honestly say I was happy. I was happy because now I had a reason to finally come to my senses and end it for good, no going back.

What I have discovered about myself is that for a long time, I didn't even notice that I was being treated badly in a romantic relationship because in that particular area my knowledge of boundaries was so low. Once this started to change and I was ready to confidently speak up for myself, this changed dramatically.

Where do these ideas come from? They often come from the people closest to you when you are growing up. It isn't always from words actually said out loud. Sometimes we infer it from the behavior of others. One client didn't think she was very intelligent because her father would tell her that she was so pretty and praise her sister for being clever. We can even get these bad impressions when in actual fact, there was a good intention behind it.

Our job now is to bust these beliefs and shine a light on them for what they are. When you put them against the actual logical truth of real life, as evidenced by things you can point to that you have done and experienced, they don't match up. It is hard to give these beliefs up though. A lot of times we hang on to them even when the evidence is right there to let go. If we let go of these stories of who we are, then it will be necessary to take risks, bust out of our comfort zone, and possibly fail at being this new person.

What you put out in your thoughts is what you will get back. Flip that script and start putting out the truth of what a totally fabulous, capable, powerful woman you are. Watch the magic that can happen for you.

Here are two great exercises to try:

1. Write down five things you tell yourself about yourself:
    I am fat and ugly, I am unlovable, I never have any money, I'll never find a good job. All men are horrible. Look at these and decide that these are not true. Decide that they are absolute rubbish! Flip the script and then write five sentences that state the truth of who you are. You can probably find actual, real-life times when the good sentences really happened!
    - I look amazing when I get up and treat myself well and put my best self forward.
    - I am a vibrant fabulous woman that people like to be around.
    - I have more than enough money to get what I need.

- I am such a great employee; anyone would be lucky to have me.
- There are plenty of great men out there just waiting for me to confidently emerge and decide that they can love me.

It seems so simple, but it can be very effective. Saying affirmations that you don't believe won't work. However, looking at the new ideas in this way will get you thinking about situations. Then, instead of looking for evidence to prove your negative thoughts, you can look for evidence of the opposite. Suddenly, instead of noticing that the boss didn't look at you as you walked past the desk today and wondering what that could mean, you notice that she smiled when you gave your opinion in the meeting this week.

2. Next time you look in the mirror and hear something nasty pop into your head or you want to apply for that new job and start to hear the story that you aren't good enough, I would like you to imagine yourself as a little girl. Look at that little girl and repeat back to her what you have just said to yourself and imagine how it is making her feel. What would the look be on her face? Do you feel bad for saying that to her? Why? There is no difference between the way you should speak to yourself or that little girl. You are both deserving of love and respect.

Now that you begin to be aware of the negative voice and the untruths it is giving you, you can start to change that story you have of who you are. Time to think about who you want to be and step out of the comfort zone to write that story for yourself instead.

Chapter 9
{ Recognizing New Relationship Dynamics }

*"Friendship is so weird... you just pick a
human you've met and you're like "yep I like
this one" and you just do stuff with them."*
– Bill Murray

When you are part of a couple for a long time, many friendships become part of your life. You add new relatives when you get married and you join communities, such as churches, together. When you are no longer part of that couple, it seems that none of your other relationships should change in too much, but this is sadly far from the case.

The relationship that will change the most, of course, is with your ex-husband. If you have been relying on him as the handyman in the home for years, it can be difficult to break the habit of asking him to help you out or have him come over and help with taxes or some other type of work that was his responsibility when you were together. I have a client who would call her ex-husband whenever she had a flat tire. Even if he is willing to help out in these areas, you need to ask yourself if you should even be asking in the first place. Is there more to this reliance? It may be that the help is going the other way. I have had clients who still feel responsible for their ex-husband. They worry about his welfare and check in on him. This can be for various reasons ranging from wanting to still be close to them to habit to guilt, but the point of fact is that they are no longer your responsibility. Holding on to these tasks may seem on the surface like a very grown up way of looking at your new relationship dynamic, but what it is actually doing is keeping you with one foot still in the marriage. It means that it is going to be very difficult to move on and start your new life. You can't live and love the life you are living now if you are holding on to the past, and you certainly can't set meaningful goals and look forward to the future.

Depending upon where you and your husband lived, you may be very close to one or another of your families or spend time traveling between the two. When you get divorced, the family of each spouse then has to come to a decision about how to view the in-law that was. If you have been good friends or close, it may seem that there is no reason to change that, but family loyalty can get very complicated. Perhaps your actual relative will be upset with you if you keep up the friendship. Either way, someone will probably feel that they have been pushed away. Along with that comes the problem of getting the children together with grandparents and the responsibility for that can get lost in the shuffle. Holiday times and vacations with the children need to be made very clear in the divorce agreement so that no one feels that they are fighting about how that will work every time it comes around.

The best way to deal with this is head-on. Without being judgmental or hostile, you will need to ask your in-laws who you wish to remain close to how they are feeling about continuing in the same way, bearing in mind that their answer may change as time goes on. Then you will have to accept their decision and try to understand that they are often in a very difficult position too. It is very easy to take this personally, but it can help to remember that this is a decision that they are basically being forced to make.

When I became divorced, I had been a part of a large in-law family who got together regularly for dinners, holidays, and vacation events. My own family was in a different country, so that meant that we were always a part of everything. Once my husband left, I was immediately cut off from the larger gatherings or any interaction with his parents. I found this very hurtful; they had been the closest thing I had to parents for about twenty years. But I did understand that, in their minds, they were being loyal to their son and the idea of their family as a unit. I did keep in touch with a couple of my sisters-in-law for quite a while, but life goes on. I was not a part of the same world anymore, so that trailed off naturally.

What this did mean for me was that I was now having the holidays with my children or alone on alternate years. In order to get through this, I had to make sure that I had new traditions with my children and found ways to make sure I was not sitting home brooding on my no-kids years. I chose to look at my time alone from the point of view as a gift of time for myself. I didn't need to cook as much (My children would never forgive me if I didn't make at least one holiday pie for every occasion). I planned in advance what I was going to do while they were gone. Sometimes I would go to a friend's house, sometimes plan a project like painting that I had wanted to do. I did volunteer a couple of times at a soup kitchen at Thanksgiving. Helping others can definitely put into perspective what you have to be grateful for in your own life.

Sometimes the relationships that you have with your own children can also change. That can be for the better in that you become closer. However, divorce can put a strain on the already difficult job of parenting. Children have to go through so many different emotions and conflicting situations during a divorce that they may blame one parent or another for it happening in the first place, whether justified or not. Add to this the job of a single parent who is stressed out and the only one around to enforce rules, then it can get quite explosive. If you can employ the help of their father to help in this area, you should reach out for that. If it becomes an area that you need to deal with by yourself, the most important thing to remember is that you cannot engage in a spiraling argument. A screaming match never solves any problems, and both sides usually dig in deeper. Depending on the age, try and listen to what they want to say to you without becoming defensive. You can respectfully disagree and tell them how they are making you feel, but often, feeling that we have been fully heard out when expressing our point of view can be all we need. Again, you really can't take too much personally when your teenager is lashing out. I can speak from experience to the fact that teenage girls can be extremely mean when they are angry or feel backed into a corner. Listen and respond quietly rather than reacting out of hurt and anger. Set boundaries, even if you think it might upset them. Very importantly, once those boundaries are set, have consequences and stick to them. Having said that, are there any areas where you could relax a little? I was so angry and stressed out by the state of my children's bedrooms that it was a constant-nagging, door-slamming conflict situation. Then I thought about how much that really mattered to me. I never went in there. They closed the door. Visitors to my home never saw them. They were happy in their squalor. I seem to remember that my room was always pretty messy growing up, and I turned out quite civilized. I decided to let it go, and they had to make sure the rest of the house was respectfully tidy. That was the end of the stress and screaming because this wasn't a big deal to me really, but I had been making it into one. Remember always that they do love you even if they are not acting like it, even if they say they don't, and even if they are being really unlovable in that moment. If you need to have them see a therapist of some kind, try to do that.

It can be very upsetting when mutual friends choose sides after your divorce. Perhaps one reason why friendships change so much after divorce is because friends aren't comfortable with grief and become rejecting or cool. Sometimes it is as simple as they just don't know what to say to you, and so the awkwardness keeps them at bay. This can also be true if they have been "couple friends." Can the woman stay with the wife and the man stay with the husband? Not really because that inevitably can cause stress in their own marriage. Because of this, generally the couple goes one way or the other.

If you are confused about the way your old relationships are changing, it can be as simple as talking to the person. Go through your contacts and assess who you think are the people you consider to be the most important to you. Who do you think can offer you the most support, positive reinforcement, and will be happy for you as you move forward with your life? Reach out to them and meet for coffee or an activity that you enjoy together. Cross off anyone who you feel will be negative about your new goals or anyone who seems more interested in the negative details of your divorce or gossiping about your ex rather than your vision for your new life.

I found that the friends that fell away after my divorce were not actually missed. My new friends are more aligned to the type of people I want to have around me. They are funny and positive and vibrant. The women who stayed with me have become even stronger friends. They have been incredibly supportive of everything I do and a huge part of my personal growth. Without them I would have found it much more difficult to stop looking back at what I thought my life was going to be, to find my passion, and to have the confidence to start my own business.

If you are feeling that your social life has disappeared after your divorce, you may find that you are feeling isolated and alone. That leads us to the question, "How do you make new friends as an adult?"

Finding friends is like dating. If you don't get out there where you can meet people that have similar interests to yours, you'll never make new friends. I understand that this can be hard. Walking up to groups of people, even in fun social situations, is very hard for me too. However, if the alternative is sitting home alone, then you need to swallow hard, slap a smile on your face, ignore the butterflies in your stomach, and introduce yourself. Easy to say but not easy to do. If you think about the worst thing that can happen when you meet new people, what would it be? They don't talk to you? They talk about stuff you can't contribute to? It's happened to me, and I felt pretty bad at the time, but I totally survived, and I'm not sure looking back that anyone else even noticed. Most of what you think is going wrong or embarrassing is part of that conversation you are having with yourself in your head. Then you walk away. You are no worse off than you were before you tried to get in on the conversation. Now think about the best-case scenario. You meet a really interesting person, become friends, have someone to pop out for coffee or a movie with. Look at it that way, and there is only an upside.

You can take a class in something you enjoy like cooking, painting, or whatever. If you look at the catalogue for both the local YMCA and your town's Parks and Recreation program, they often have community classes that are relatively inexpensive, and the people who go there will be in your area. Another great resource you can check out is the local library as they have lots of activities posted for the town.

Get involved in a church group or some other group that meets regularly. You could even join a gym.

Reaching out to a community of other divorced women is also very helpful because not only do they understand what you are going through, but they are probably looking to make new friends, too; an easy way to do this is through groups that can be found on Facebook's events section. If you can google Meet-Up, or even download their app, they have an amazing array of all kinds of activities you didn't even know you were interested in but may now want to try!

Take every opportunity that comes along, rather than deciding to hide out in your house. Even work events might lead to meeting new people. I met my best after-divorce friend because a married neighbor of mine knew that we were both going through our divorces at the same time and thought we would have things in common. It was so nice to have someone who understood what I was going through. Yes, we talked about the rotten parts about being divorced and whined a little, but mostly we got each other out of the house to have fun.

Chapter 10
Focus on Your
Goals and Passions

"It always seems impossible until it's done."
– Nelson Mandela

U p until this point you have worked through all those things that have been holding you back. Finally, you are seeing yourself for who you truly are. You have changed the story of yourself from the one that had been given to you by others to the one that you want to live. From this place, it becomes much easier to think about what you want for your life going forward. As caretakers of children, husbands, the home, work, and others we felt somehow responsible for, there has never been time to actually think about what you want out of life. When I have the initial call with my clients and ask them what their goals for the future are, without exception they realize that this is a question that they don't really know how to answer. It is usually very surprising to them that they don't know the answer to this. They become frustrated and apologetic, and I have to reassure them that this isn't some glaring flaw they have. The reason, of course, that they don't know what to say is that it is a question that has never really been asked of them, even by themselves. There has been no time to contemplate what they want out of life. The focus has always been on what others need.

So now this is your time to focus on what you want to do and who you want to be in this new life you have started. There is generally some feeling of guilt that can accompany this part of the process, the guilt that we are being selfish by focusing on ourselves and our wants. Some of this is habit; some of it is the ingrained feeling that we must always be there for other people. I have had several clients tell me that this is the model that they saw from their own mother, and it was hard to think that there was a different way. The most important thing to remember at this point, however, is that you cannot be there for other people if you are not your best self. As they tell you every time you get on an airplane, in the event of an emergency, put the oxygen mask on yourself before helping others. If you don't, you may not survive to be around to help someone else, or you may flounder around and do a sloppy job of it, leaving them to struggle. Or as RuPaul says, "If you can't love yourself, how are you gonna love somebody else?"

Previously, we looked at ending the unkind things that we say to ourselves, this is the time to add to this idea by treating ourselves well physically, mentally, and spiritually. One way to do this is to make yourself a list of activities that nurture you, not from a hunger for food standpoint but rather nourishment of your soul. You can put all kinds of things on the list. Some could be things that you consider an extravagant treat for special occasions, like going to a spa day. Others could be every day activities, like carving out time to walk your dog outside in nature. Anything that makes you feel refreshed and whole, less stressed and happy can go on your list. Post it somewhere where you can readily see it and add to it as things occur to you. That way, when there are times that you feel overwhelmed or emotionally drained, it will be easy to find and pick something to do to refresh yourself.

Some great examples to get you started might be:

- Yoga
- Meditation
- Warm bath/shower
- Walk outside
- Spend time with a pet
- Mani/pedi appointment
- Talk on the phone to a good friend
- Painting, gardening, fishing (any hobby you love to do)
- Exercising
- Journaling

Spending time doing things for yourself will also go a long way to convincing yourself of how important you are. Once you truly understand that you are worth nurturing and investing time and energy in, then you will find that a feeling of self-confidence will easily follow. That confidence is all you need to push past the fears that are holding you back and allow you to break out of the comfort zone of your past. Onwards and upwards!

Who is it you want to be in this new life? That is a very different question to what it is you want to do. If someone were to describe you, what would you like them to say about you? I have met so many women who have introduced themselves to me as so and so's mom or wife. It can almost be as if they are erasing themselves without even realizing it. Their accomplishments and who they are isn't important. You can still be somebody's mother, or aunt, or even girlfriend, but what do you actually want people you know to say about you? A great exercise to do here is pick three qualities you want to have (confidence, for example). Then pick three words to describe those qualities (confident). Write down your three words and post them somewhere you see them. Sit with them for a couple of days and really decide if this is how you would like people to describe you. Once you are sure, then as you go about you day from then on, try to live up to being that person. Look for evidence that you are doing things in your life that someone with those qualities would do.

Now that you are revved up and raring to move on to your new fabulous life, it is time to figure out what it is you want to do there! Finding your passions will let you know which direction to go in. To do this, you can ask a series of questions that will remind you of what you love about life. Go back to when you were a child and think about what you loved to do more than anything else. Write that on your list, even if it was to ride your bike down the street. Is there anything that you do now that makes you lose track of time? I know that when my children were young I didn't read as much as I would have liked to because once I got engrossed, it seemed that it was suddenly very late and there were some hungry kids wondering where dinner was. What does that for you? Imagine that you had some magic elixir that meant you could do anything you liked with guaranteed success, what would you do? Is there any activity you do that just makes you feel so amazing about yourself? Something that you feel you could teach to others? What about if you let go of the judgement of others? What then would be the first thing that you would do? You just won the lottery and money is no object, so how would you spend your time? Write down three people that you admire the most and why they inspire you. Think about your best quality and how it might inspire others. Lastly, if you knew you only had one day left to live, what would be the biggest regret about something you didn't do in life?

Really take a long time to consider each of these questions. Eventually that should give you a list of insights about things you love about life. You will no doubt find a common thread when you consider all the answers carefully. This will point you to what you hold dear and include in your life moving forward.

You can incorporate all of this so far in your daily life and habits, and the outward actions will soon be inward manifestations of you living the life you want. Now you are in a space to truly appreciate the amazing things that you already have in your day to day life. Even little things like noticing that the weather was warmer today than yesterday can become a cause for gratitude.

I love to have my clients make a bucket list of things that they want to do. They can put anything on that list, whether they think it is possible or not. It can range from taking a cruise to the Mediterranean, to learning to tango, to meditating for five minutes per day. You can create your own list and keep it posted somewhere handy. Having small items that you can tick off easily is a great way to reconnect with who you are and begin seeing yourself as separate from your ex. It's also great for building confidence in your abilities and taking care of yourself.

If you need support in this, you could find a friend to do it with you or engage a coach so they can help with encouragement, accountability, and celebrate your successes.

What would be on your list?

I have a client who was feeling that she was the cause of all the pain that her children were going through from the divorce. She initiated it because she was living a life that was very unhappy for her, but nonetheless, she could not shake the guilt that she had let her family down. She said that she was extremely depressed and trapped in fact she told me that she hated herself. She felt so guilty and worthless. Added to that, she had a job that she liked, but it was stressful. She did not love or even feel comfortable in what she was doing because, she came to realize, she was allowing the judgement of others to stand in the way. Once she had come to realize her own importance, things started to change pretty rapidly. Not only did she decide that it was only important what she thought about what she was doing and so was able to change her work situation, but she was then able to express what her true passion in life was. I was surprised to find out that she had written and illustrated several children's books. Expressing herself in this form was her passion, yet she had literally hidden this all away in a box so that no one else could see it. She realized that she wanted to work with children and enable them to express themselves through art too. She had never had the confidence to believe that any of this was possible when she was hiding in that dark emotional place. Today, she is proudly sharing her books, and she has a beautiful studio where she teaches art. She is living her passion and setting goals for her future. Only three months before she began, that had seemed an impossibility to her.

Setting smaller goals on a regular basis will keep you on track to where you want to go now, from intending to exercise three times a week to making sure that you get the promotion that is up for grabs at work. I am a huge list maker, which is quite interesting when you know that I used to make fun of my ex-husband for making lists for everything. I love them so much as a technique for getting things done and feeling a sense of accomplishment that I sometimes put on things that I have done, just so I can show them crossed off.

Once you know what it is that makes you happy, maybe you are finding things every day to live your passion in life. It doesn't have to be a radical new step like changing careers. That is not always possible or even necessary. If you love to paint, you don't have to be an art teacher, you can just make sure that you set time aside to do that, or you can donate time at a local school. There are many ways to live your passion; knowing it and expressing it is the main thing. Finally, you need to set goals for your new life. These will be constantly changing and evolving. There are major life goals, like where to live, what to do to make money (this is where knowing your passions comes in handy), or how do you want to live your life and the type of person you want to be. It is worth taking the time and setting down on paper the answers to those, and some of it you will already know from the exercises above. If you have a concrete plan written down, it will help you to focus on what you really want. It is also worth looking over them every year or so to see if you feel the same way.

Once you have decided on these goals, you need to come up with an action plan of how you are going to get there. Using my artist client as an example, she had the goal of a children's art studio, but she then had to make it happen. There was a business name to consider, where she would choose to do this, how she was going to organize the classes, equipment she needed to get, and how this was going to work around her full-time job that she wasn't ready to give up just yet. Brainstorming the path that you need to get you to your goal could feel overwhelming, and the old, less confident you might have been inclined to throw up your hands and say it's never going to work. Remember, this is fear talking to you. Instead, look at your list and choose the first and easiest thing you can do. Only once that is well on the way or accomplished do you need to worry about the next thing. Bite-sized mini-goals will get you to the bigger accomplishment on your path to this fabulous life you are setting up for yourself.

{ **Chapter 11**
Obstacles }

"If you find a path with no obstacles,
it probably doesn't lead anywhere."
– Frank A. Clark

I looked up the word "obstacle" in the Oxford dictionaries as I was beginning to write this chapter. The official definition is "a thing that blocks one's way or prevents or hinders progress." Think about what could possibly be blocking your way to move on to the future that you deserve. In answering that question, we also might want to think about who or what is throwing those blockages in to your path. If you are sitting back now and making your list of all the "others" that you can point to in answer to that, then you should make sure to leave a space for your own name at the very top of that list. This may seem harsh, and you may think I'm victim blaming. However, even if the divorce, any financial hardship, or harassment that you are dealing with now was totally, one hundred percent on someone else, taking action to improve your life and future is one hundred percent in your hands now.

I have spoken to many women that think the best option to solving the problems they face after their divorce is to find a new relationship. It would seem to take care of issues of self-esteem, finance, social activities, and loneliness for a start. I see the logic in that line of thinking. The problem with that is for many it actually leads to greater feelings of low self-worth and rarely turns out for the best. I say many because I do know friends who met and married a wonderful man fairly soon after divorce. I thought I was going down that path myself at one point. It didn't turn out well for me or for many women that I have spoken to.

There are so many reasons to block you in this area, but the main one I have found is the way we see ourselves and expect to be treated after the end of a marriage. If boundaries, expectations and feelings of confidence and self-worth are all pretty low, the impression we are sending out to the world in general is that we don't deserve too much respect. Even though it is never acknowledged, somehow the perfect fit to your damage is out there with his own damage, and you fit together perfectly, like a jigsaw.

But a jigsaw causes you more pain than happiness. That is a pretty big generalization but one that I have found to be true in my clients (and myself at one point). The way this plays out is that even if we do feel in our gut that something isn't right with this man or this relationship, we ignore it. We make excuses. That red flag? Well we make excuses for the behavior, sometimes even feel like the poor man has had such a difficult time, he can't help being that way. Then there is always the thought in the back of your head that he is better than no one. Very often, it seems just like you are back in the same bad relationship that you had in the past. The solution to this is to wait. Wait until you are ready to send out into the world the confidence and feeling that you are worth treating well, that you will not put up with bad treatment, and that you are a capable woman in her own right. That will create a completely different kind of relationship.

My client Jean met a new man soon after her divorce when she was feeling vulnerable. He was charming and took her out and was far nicer to her than her ex-husband had ever been. However, a couple of months into the relationship, he had to travel away for work and told her that it would be better to break up as he would be gone several months. Jean was devastated, but what could she do? Three months later, he was back in town for his work in that part of the country, so he called her. She readily agreed to start up again. She thought they had a wonderful time. Until, of course, it was time for him to take his seasonal job to a different place again. He left and never contacted her during the next few months. The new season rolled around again and... you see the rest I'm sure. All this was taking a toll on Jean. She had started a new relationship, but when the man rolled into town again, he had convinced her to see him instead. She was totally confused by his behavior but couldn't get herself to shut him out. Finally by the third round, she did—until she saw him later in a local grocery store, which prompted her to text him and off they went again. I asked Jean what she would advise a good friend who was trapped in this relationship to do. Her answer was to tell her friend to never see this man again. With support, that is what Jean was able to do. She worked hard on the things about herself that had made it possible to allow herself to be treated this way. So now instead of that being her obstacle, it is her learning tool that pushed her to improve life and move on to a more positive future.

Not being able to let go of the past or your ex-husband is a huge stumbling block. It can come in two forms. He won't let you forget he is out there with constant contact or behavior that leads you to react negatively, or it can be that you are holding on to old habits, like expecting him to fix things around the house. You may be snooping into what he is doing now, or who he has a relationship with. I covered how you can change these reactions in an earlier chapter. Something I hear quite regularly when talking to women after their divorce is that they still love their ex-husband so much and that is why they can't let go. How do you stop emotions that have been a part of your life for such a long time? The answer is, of course, that you can't just cut them off. That person is always going to be a huge part of who you are in some form or another. So, go ahead and acknowledge that. However, holding on to the idea that you are still in love with him is really a part of your comfort zone, and you can work through that. An exercise I have my clients do may help to put perspective on this for you.

Take a sheet of paper and draw three vertical columns. At the top of the first, write, "Ways I was treated during marriage/ how it made me feel." At the top of the second, "Ways I was treated during and after divorce/ how it made me feel." At the top of the third, "What is love/ how you should feel." Fill in these columns one at a time. Once you have finished, look over them very carefully and see if it helps you at all.

If you have children of any age, the chances are that you will need to be connected to your ex on some level and probably have to go to functions where he is present also. For the sanity of your children, keeping this as civil and pleasant as possible is always a good idea. Children of any age can have behavior that causes us pain, both emotionally and financially. Issues with your children, whether caused by the divorce or not, can be another reason we have for not looking after ourselves and holding back from moving on. As mothers, we feel very responsible for our children. We take on their pain, try to solve their problems, and fix what we see as wrong in their lives to a greater or lesser extent. At some point though, holding on to control over the lives of older children can become a tool that we are using to hide from our own needs, problems and fears that we don't want to face. Getting involved in the relationship they have with their father, for instance, probably isn't helping anyone. In fact, it is possibly causing harm to most. In particular, it is causing you to become enveloped in drama with your ex and gives you the excuse that you have to stay in that place "for your children."

This is a painful time in life, and no one can be blamed for wanting to fix the way you feel as quickly as possible. Buying lots of books and looking for one person to magically help you is tempting, but the truth is that the person to help you the most is yourself. Yes, you can listen to good advice and go out and find support and accountability, this makes the odds of you succeeding improve infinitely. Yet, if you are not willing to face your reality and commit to wanting to move on, then things will not change very much. It is so much easier to use all the excuses that are readily available to you. It is so much easier to blame those that have wronged you. Fear of what may be out there in your new life is a powerful block. How much easier to stay right where you are, where you know what is happening at this moment. If you don't try to break out and do something different, you can't mess it up. That way you get to keep blaming all those others. If you don't try something new, no one can judge you. No one will say "I told you so" when things don't work out. Doing the work that you will need to do to help yourself and get to where you want to go is not easy.

That is why I say your biggest obstacle in this process is you.

{ Chapter 12
What's Next for You? }

"It's ok to be scared. Being scared means you're
about to do something really, really brave."
— Mandy Hale

Every story of life before marriage, life during marriage, and the experience of the divorce is different. Whole life experience is what brings us all to this place at this time. A common theme that comes up over and over after midlife divorce, however, is the feeling that we are in a place that we didn't think we would ever be. Add to that the fear that we have no idea how to positively move on to get stability and control over life as it is now. It is overwhelming when thinking about where to start and trusting that we can make the correct decisions even if we believe that we have a goal in mind. What brings together the women that I have spoken to and those that I have been privileged to work with is the decision to make a commitment to change from within. That is what ultimately led them to change the life that they live now and the fabulous future that they can see for themselves.

The women who can use the seven key steps to allow themselves to step out of the comfort zone and take a look at those things that are holding them back are the women who will thrive rather than just survive. This is not something that you need to necessarily do in a linear order. There will be days when you might want to think about aspects of more than one step at a time.

Looking back at your marriage from a place of curiosity can help you to see a clearer picture of what it was really like. Thinking about the woman you were in the marriage and the woman that you would like to be can help you to let go of the past and instead focus on the future. Remembering that no one has control over what another person ultimately does will help you to understand that there wasn't some magic thing you should have done to stop this happening. If it was really the life you should have been living, then that is where you would be. Make the next phase of your life the life you should be living.

Facing fears about finances by looking at the reality of your situation will help you to lessen the anxiety you are having over it. When you know the truth of your situation, then you can take action to get yourself to a better place and more in line with where you want to be.

Burying your emotions with food or shopping or whatever else you may have identified as a way for you to avoid the pain of your divorce will eventually only lead to greater problems while the things you don't want to face are not going to go away. Instead, they are going to grow, even if only in your mind. That anxiety and fear will always be playing in the background like an annoying song on the radio that you can't stop humming. Look for positive habits instead and be aware of things that are triggering you to run to the cookie jar.

If you can let go of the past and stop the blame game by learning to forgive, life will immediately open up so much more for you. Living with anger, guilt, regret and sadness can become your uncomfortable comfort zone. It is your mind's way of keeping you safe from venturing out past the fear barrier to what may be next. Learning to respond rather than react to what others are doing will help you feel calm and in control of the situation. Gratitude for what you have right now can help to put everything into perspective.

Recognize the way that you think about yourself, and that view that you project out in to the world will impact every aspect of your life. Once you can figure out where the false beliefs you hold about yourself come from, then replacing them with the reality of who you are will be more successful. Once you can acknowledge your achievements and strengths and really believe them, confidence follows. This is a never-ending process because you can build on that to choose who it is you want to be going forward.

Finding out who your friends are, literally, is a big part of divorce. Instead of viewing this from a negative standpoint, you can use it to reassess who you want to have around you. What are the values that you think are important? Are any of these people causing you to feel badly about yourself? This is an opportunity for you to get out and do activities you love and be with amazing people that support and inspire you.

Finally, you are ready to decide what you want to do with this new life. I love to describe every new step in life as the next great adventure. After spending time looking after everyone else, there seemed to be no time to have ever thought about what it is you like or want. No one ever asked or cared, including yourself. First, you can find your passion so that a bigger picture of what you want to do can emerge. Then set bite sized goals for yourself that will move your life forward to live your fabulous future.

My own great adventure continues every day. I went from that fearful place to feeling in control over where my life is and where it is heading. I am a very different person from who I was ten years ago. I am calmer and less reactive and angry. My anger was not even from my divorce but something that had been there for a very long time before that. My habit of being attracted to "interesting" people as friends and romantic partners has been broken. I realized that interesting actually meant being toxic and surrounded by drama. This was my way of staying close to the comfort zone of my childhood while telling myself that I had moved away from that. I wake up every day and spend the first ten minutes before I open my eyes thinking about all the fabulous possibilities that could happen that day. This is where I want you to be. Excited for the day every day when you get up, in the space where you are looking forward to the next phase of your life, loving the person that you are now and understanding your boundaries, being able to handle to stresses that life throws at you and not letting them send you into a tailspin, not being financially stressed out because now you have the confidence to figure out how you are going to get yourself into a financially stable place.

I'm really nothing special or different from you. I was blindsided by a divorce at age forty-four with four children in a country without any of my own family around me. Most of our friends were people my ex had grown up with or gone to college with. I had been a stay-at-home mother. I was terrified to be on my own. How would I manage my finances and pay bills, figure out where to live, deal with a house on my own, and what about my children? This is how I know you can do this.

I leave you here with a good sense that there is a clear path to get to the place where you feel secure and in control of your life.

As one of my clients wrote, "The differences that I see in myself after working with you is a more confident woman who has slowed down to take care of myself, nourish myself, and appreciate the unique differences in who I am. I catch myself when I start judging myself or others, and I lead out of a sense of empowerment and expectation that others will hear what I have to say or there will be consequences. I have a deep sense of peace that I haven't had in a long time. I so wanted to be in the state I am now, full of peace and able to manage the negative beliefs, but not sure I thought it was possible. So, I am surprised by the amount we accomplished. I also found it surprising how well you listened and caught things I said, then found exercises and actions to help. I loved your drive and desire to see me succeed."

I would love to hear from you about your journey from Fearful to Fabulous and the best thing about your new life. Feel free to shoot me an email at fiona@findfabulouswithfiona.com

You may be wondering, however, how you are going to be able to follow through with all of this great information. You probably have questions about how you'll be able to put these steps into your life effectively. Maybe you realize that you are in need of support.

If that is the case, then I would love to share more with you!

I'm offering a free forty-five-minute Discovery Call in which we can find out what is holding you back or slowing you down from getting where you want to be. Let's discover how I can help you implement the steps outlined in this book that are most relevant to you. Just plug this link into your browser to set up our call: https://Findyourfabulouswholeself.as.me/DiscoveryCall

Further Reading

The Big Leap by Gay Hendricks
The 5 Second Rule by Mel Robbins
10 Percent Happier by Dan Harris
-And any book written by Jennifer Sincero

Acknowledgments

I came to this amazing place where I could step out of my own fear and feel that I could make a difference with the help of other women who had blasted through their own life challenges to make a difference to others. I must thank some other coaches that I have met who became firm friends and inspired me to keep going when I things did not always work out the way I wanted: Amber, Susan, and Kavetha were in this group, even though they may not know the help they have given me. I must also thank my good friend Deb Friedman, who suggested I should branch out and be a coach in the first place. It was a winding journey from my initial "Is that a real thing that people do?" to where I am now. Also, a special thanks to my own (tough-love) coach Belinda Ginter who didn't allow me to hide who I truly was and made sure that I put on my big girl pants and stilettos to get out there and make a difference.

Very importantly, thank you to my children who listened to me daily talking about what I needed to do, what I had done, and needing to tiptoe around the house if I was trying to write, coach, make videos, or listen to training for myself. On the occasions that dinner didn't get made until late or not at all, they got it together themselves with no complaining. Their support and apparently doubtless assumption that I was definitely capable of writing a book helped me to actually believe myself that I could actually write a book.

I want to acknowledge my mother. She, sadly, did not move on from an unlivable situation in her marriage to find her true worth and new life. However, two weeks before she died, she opened up to me about feeling she had wasted her life and wishing she had had the strength to change it. That was a powerful statement, one which took a lot of courage to make. It has stuck with me for the past twenty-two years, and I believe it has helped me to make the changes I have made in my own life. The changes that ultimately led me to write this book. I also believe that was her intention.

Thank you to my Morgan James Publishing Team: David Hancock, CEO & Founder; my Author Relations Manager, Margo Toulouse, and special thanks to Jim Howard, Bethany Marshall, and Nickcole Watkins.

Thank You

Thank you so much for reading through this book!

Not only because you took the time to read what I wrote but because you are taking the steps to find your power, move on, and thrive. Helping you find your way to do this is my passion and purpose.

If you want to find out if you are still struggling with your Divorce Hangover- more importantly, if you are ready to cure that and move on, take my on-line Quiz at

https://findfabulouswithfiona.com/your-divorce-hangover-cure-quiz/

Love,

Fiona

About the Author

Fiona Eckersley is an Author, Confidence Coach, and Divorce Recovery Expert. She works with women in their forties and beyond who are struggling with the challenges of divorce and fears about to how to move on and thrive in their new reality.

Originally from the North of England, she has been in the United States for almost thirty years. Fiona had worked in Great Britain, Sierra Leone, and the United States during her earlier career as a teacher. While married, she stayed home to raise her four children.

When she was forty-four years old and married for seventeen years, she learned that her whole life was about to be flipped upside down and the future that she had thought was fixed was going to be completely different.

The next several years were a bumpy, eye opening, impactful, tearful, inspirational, and totally amazing ride.

During that time, after many missteps, Fiona learned to overcome her own self-limiting, negative thoughts, emotional blocks, and incorrect beliefs.

Today Fiona is a certified coach who has found her passion helping her clients regain their confidence and blast through their own fears and challenges brought on by midlife divorce. She lives in Connecticut by the beach with her two extremely spoiled dogs and her youngest daughter, who will soon be off to college.

Findfabulouswithfiona.com

fiona@findfabulouswithfiona.com

https://www.facebook.com/fabwithfiona/

https://www.instagram.com/fab.with.fiona/

https://twitter.com/fabwithfiona

https://Findyourfabulouswholeself.as.me/DiscoveryCall

Printed in the USA
CPSIA information can be obtained
at www.ICGtesting.com
JSHW080001150824
68134JS00021B/2209

9 781642 797039